EP Math 3

Parent's Guide

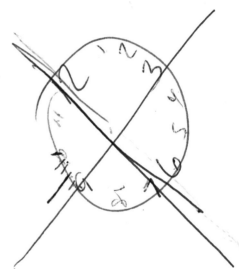

Welcome to the EP Math 3 Parent's Guide!

This little book was created to help you go offline while following EP's Math 3 curriculum. You will need the EP Math 3 student workbook for your child. Without the online lessons, you will need to be your child's teacher. The directions are here for introducing new topics. The workbook will provide practice and review.

This book also includes objectives for each lesson, materials marked where needed, directions for what to do each lesson, and the complete answer key.

There are lessons when the students are told to color something, so crayons are listed as a material needed. However, they could just color those things in with their pencil if need be.

They will be learning their multiplication and division facts this year. You might want to have a place where you hang up the "fact of the day" and recruit family members to randomly quiz your child on it.

And a little note: To avoid calling all children "he" or the awkward phrasing of "him or her," I've used the plural pronoun when referring to your child, such as, "Show the clock to your child and have them point to the hour hand."

Have a great year.

Lee

Review

These first lessons I'm not having you introduce the topics because it's supposed to be review. If your child needs more practice on something, take the time to work on it a little.

Lesson 1

- Students will: use number sequencing to fill in missing numbers, compare numbers, draw shapes
- Take a look at the hundreds chart at the beginning of your book. Have your child see how the tens stay the same in each row and the ones stay the same in each column.
- Lesson 1 worksheet
  - Talk over the worksheet with your child before they begin.
    - Part A: The top is like a hundreds chart, but just pieces of it. A blank box before a number should be filled in with the number that comes before it. A blank box after a number should be filled in with the number that comes next.
    - Part B: Ask your child which end of the greater than/less than symbol points to the bigger number and the smaller number.
    - Part C: Your child may not know all the shapes they are supposed to draw. You can tell them the number of sides and use the answer key to show them as well.

Lesson 2 (Legos or such, if needed, for practicing tens and ones)

- Students will: use problem solving to fill in the missing addends, identify numbers by ones and tens
- Lesson 2 worksheet
  - Again, you can use the worksheet to review with your child.
    - Part A: In the first section they will balance the scale by filling in numbers that when added together will equal the number on the other side.
    - Part B: In the second part they will just be counting blocks. If they don't remember tens and ones blocks, you can get Legos out and build towers of tens with blocks left over and count them up.
      - You can remind them that in their answer the one digit shows the number of tens and the other shows the number of ones.

Lesson 3 (brown crayon, inch ruler, coins if you like)

- Students will: add the value of coins, measure inches with a ruler, read analog clocks to the quarter hour
- Lesson 3 worksheet
  - Go over the worksheet with your child. (continued on next page)

- Part A: If your child isn't confident with the coins, get some out and practice identifying and adding them before trying the worksheet.
  - The directions tell them to color the pennies brown.
- Part B: The second part requires a ruler. Remind your child to start at the 0 marking, not the end of the ruler. They are measuring in inches.
- Part C: The third part is about reading clocks to :15, :30, and :45.
  - If they aren't confident, use the clocks below to review.
    - Count the minutes by five while pointing to the numbers around the clock.
    - Ask your child to identify the minute and hour hand.
    - Remind your child that the hour is the number the hour hand has passed.
  - Ask your child to read the time.

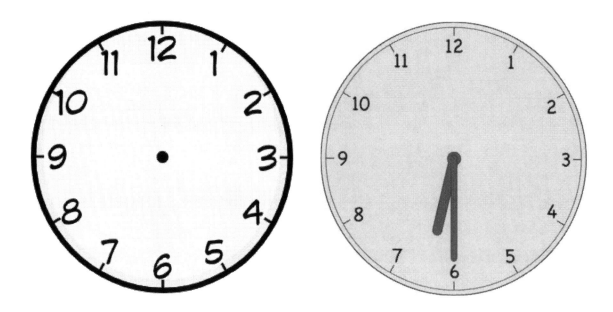

Lesson 4

- Students will: read a tally chart to answer questions, use tens and ones to identify numbers
- Lesson 4 worksheet
  - Go over the worksheet with your child before they begin to make sure they understand what to do.
    - Tally marks are a way of recording a number. They asked people a question and made a mark for each answer. At the end we can easily count up how many there are by counting by fives and ones.
    - Show your child what five looks like (Thursday).
    - Have your child tell you how many voted for each day.

Lesson 5
- Students will: count by twos and write even numbers, identify numbers written as hundreds, tens, and ones
- Lesson 5 worksheet
    - Part A
        - Ask your child what kind of numbers are labeled on the snail.
            - even
        - They will count forward and backward by two to write the numbers by the dots. They will only be writing even numbers.
    - Part B: For the second part of the page ask your child how many blocks they would have if they had a big block made of four hundred blocks, a block made of thirty blocks, and eight other blocks. (This is the first problem.)
        - 438
        - They will match the numbers to their expanded form, showing their hundreds, tens, and ones.

Lesson 6
- Students will: find numbers that come before and after, write digits in their proper place value, add 11
- Turn back to your hundreds chart at the beginning of the book.
    - Add ten to numbers. Have your child put their finger on any number and jump down one line. That's adding ten. Do several numbers.
    - Now add eleven.
        - Jump down one row and over one. Try several numbers.
        - What's the answer each time?
            - It's one more ten and one more one.
            - $23 + 11 = 34$ ($2 + 1 = 3$ and $3 + 1 = 4$)
- Lesson 6 worksheet
    - Part A: Write in the numbers that come before and after.
    - Part B: They can write any number that fits the description.
        - 70, 73, 77, 79, etc.
        - 32, 2, 82, etc.
        - 100, 199, etc.
    - Part C: Add 11 in the hundreds chart puzzle pieces.
- Make sure your child is keeping up with facts learning. They should know addition and subtraction easily at this point. Use flashcards, quizzing, online games, or our facts books to help you.

Lesson 7
- Students will: write multiples of ten, add multiples of ten onto double digit numbers using visual cues and vertical addition problems
- Go back to the hundreds chart at the beginning of the book.
    - Ask your child to point to any number on the thirties row.
    (continued on the next page)

- o Ask your child to add ten.
  - ▪ They should jump forward one row and say the answer.
- o Have your child go back to the first number and add twenty this time.
  - ▪ They should jump forward two rows and say the answer.
- o Repeat this with thirty and forty if you are having fun. ☺
- Lesson 7 worksheet
  - o Part A: To add the blocks, they just need to count the tens and then count the ones and write down the totals.
  - o Part B: They will just count by tens and fill in the spaces.
  - o Part C: They will answer the addition problems by adding vertically. You can show them how they are adding the tens and adding the ones.

Review: Adding with Regrouping

Lesson 8 (Legos or other such block to practice regrouping with manipulatives – 23 if you can – You could even make chains of paper clips.)
- Students will: add with regrouping
- Use Legos to add together 7 and 8. Build a tower of ten and then count what's left over. (You could also draw pictures.)
  - o 1 ten, 5 ones, 15
  - o Write the problem vertically on a piece of paper.
    - ▪ There are no tens so the ten you just made is adding to nothing and is just one in the answer.
- Do the same with 15 and 8 more blocks.
  - o Build a second tower of ten. Count the tens and the ones.
    - ▪ 2 tens, 3 ones, 23
    - ▪ Write this problem vertically on a piece of paper.
      - Five plus eight is thirteen. There is one ten and three ones in thirteen.
      - You write the three in the ones column and then you have to add the one ten onto the tens column. Show your child how to write a one above the tens column. (You can see an example in the workbook.)
      - Then add the tens, 1 + 1, and get 2 for the tens column.
      - 2 tens, 3 ones, 23
- Lesson 8 worksheet
  - o Part A: Your child can count the blocks to find the answer.
  - o Part B: Go over the first problem with your child. 24 + 8. Ask your child what 4 + 8 is.
    - ▪ 12
    - ▪ Ask your child where the twelve is on the page.
      - The 2 is under the eight and the one is above the two.
      - Why?
        - o Have your child make 12 with blocks, 1 ten and 2 ones. (continued on the next page)

- Show your child how you write the ones in the ones column and you add the ten into the tens column.
        - Watch your child get started on these to make sure they are being done correctly.
    - Part C: Not all of these need regrouping and there is no box to use. If there are no extra tens to add, they shouldn't add them!
- Don't forget to be working on math facts.

Lesson 9
- Students will: add with regrouping
- Lesson 9 worksheet
    - This is similar to Lesson 8's worksheet.

Lesson 10
- Students will: solve addition word problems with regrouping
- Lesson 10 worksheet
    - They should read the stories, write the numbers and addition problems.
    - Have your child make up a problem for you to make sure they understand what they mean.

Review: Subtraction

Lesson 11
- Students will: counting backward by ten, subtract by ten
- Go to the hundreds chart in the beginning of your book.
    - Have your child choose a number and then subtract ten. How would they do that?
        - They would jump up a row. (ie. 34 to 24)
        - You can have your child try other numbers and see how fast they can tell you the answer.
- Lesson 11 worksheet
- Show your child the different parts of the worksheet before they begin.
    - Part A: They will use the picture to subtract by ten. They can cross off a group of ten to show it is being subtracted and then count what's left of the first number.
    - Part B: They will count backward by tens from 90.
    - Part C: Subtract ten using vertical problems. Show them they are subtracting zero ones, so the ones digit stays the same. Then they are subtracting the tens digits straight down.

Lesson 12
- Students will: subtract single digits from double digits
- Lesson 12 worksheet
    - Show your child the different parts of the worksheet before they begin.
    - Part A: They will use the picture to subtract. They can cross off the number of blocks that are being subtracted from the first number.
    - Part B: Subtract using vertical problems. Show them they are subtracting the ones straight down. There are no tens in the bottom number, so they are subtracting nothing from the number of tens. The tens number will stay the same.

Lesson 13
- Students will: subtract double digits from double digits without regrouping
- Lesson 13 worksheet
- Show your child the different parts of the worksheet before they begin.
    - Part A: They will use the picture to subtract. They can cross off the number of blocks that are being subtracted from the first number.
    - Part B: Subtract using vertical problems. Show them they are subtracting the ones straight down and then the tens.

Subtraction with Regrouping

Lesson 14 (Legos or such)
- Students will: subtract by two with an introduction to regrouping
- Make a tower of ten Legos along with a few individual Lego blocks. Subtract seven.
    - Have your child figure out how to take away seven blocks, and ask them to explain what happened. How many tens and ones were there? How many tens and ones are there after you subtracted seven?
    - They had to take away the group of ten by breaking it up. They started with one ten and ended up with no groups of ten. The leftover pieces became ones.
- Write the problem 23 – 7 vertically.
    - Ask your child if you can take 7 away from 3.
        - no
    - Ask your child where you can get more from so that you can subtract 7. (Hint: Think Legos or whatever you were just using.)
    - You are going to break up a stack of ten into ones. Those ten "blocks" are going to move from the tens column into the ones column because we need them there to take away the seven needed.
        - Cross off the two and make it a one.
            - You took away a stack of ten. You broke it up into ones, so you can take away seven blocks.
            (continued on the next page)

- That ten is going to move to the ones column. Write a one next to the three. It's now thirteen. Three plus ten is thirteen. We didn't subtract anything yet. We just moved ten "blocks" from one place to another.
  - Now, they can take 7 away from 13. What's the answer?
    - 6
  - There is just one left and you are subtracting nothing from it, so the answer is one ten and six ones, sixteen.
- Lesson 14 worksheet
  - Part A: Have your child cross off the number of blocks being subtracted. They will have to cross off some from a group of ten which will turn the rest into ones.
  - Part B: Count back by twos.
  - Part C: Subtract two. Some will require regrouping.
    - They can subtract straight down. If they can't take two away (from one or zero), they will have to take away one of the tens and break it into ones.
    - Of course, to subtract two they can count back two, just like counting backward by two.
    - Have your child circle the problems that required regrouping, where the number of tens changed.

Lesson 15 (Legos or such)
- Students will: subtract one digit from two digits with regrouping
- Make a tower of ten Legos along with a few individual Lego blocks. Subtract seven.
  - Have your child figure out how to take away seven blocks, and ask them to explain what happened. How many tens and ones were there? How many tens and ones are there after you subtracted seven?
  - They had to take away the group of ten by breaking it up. They started with one ten and ended up with no groups of ten. The leftover pieces became ones.
- Write the problem 25 – 8 vertically.
  - Ask your child if you can take 8 away from 5.
    - no
  - Ask your child where you can get more from so that you can subtract 8. (Hint: Think Legos or whatever you were just using.)
  - You are going to break up a stack of ten into ones. Those ten "blocks" are going to move from the tens column into the ones column because we need them there to take away the eight needed.
    - Cross off the two and make it a one.
      - You took away a stack of ten. You broke it up into ones, so you can take away eight blocks.
        (continued on the next page)

- That ten is going to move to the ones column. Write a one next to the five. It's now fifteen. Five plus ten is fifteen. We didn't subtract anything yet. We just moved ten "blocks" from one place to another.
    - Now, they can take 8 away from 15. What's the answer?
        - 7
    - There is just one ten left and you are subtracting nothing from it, so the answer is one ten and seven ones, seventeen.
- Lesson 15 worksheet
    - Part A: Have your child cross off the number of blocks being subtracted. They will have to cross off some from a group of ten which will turn the rest into ones.
    - Part B: Subtract with regrouping. Talk through the example 63 – 9.
        - Can you take nine away from three?
            - no
        - What do you need to do?
            - Take a group of ten and move it to the ones.
        - Cross of the six and make it a five.
            - There were six groups of ten. Now there are five groups of ten. Where did the ten go?
        - Write a one next to the three.
            - Now there are thirteen ones. How do you subtract now?
                - 13 – 9 = 4
                - Write four in the ones column where the answer goes.
            - Then subtract the tens. There are no tens being subtracted from five tens.
                - 5 – 0 = 5
        - The answer is five tens and four ones, 54.
        - You could watch your child do the first problem, but don't direct them. If they have a question, refer to the example about what the next step is.
    - Part C: Subtract. Some will need regrouping, some not.

Lesson 16 (Legos or such if you can gather more than 20)
- Students will: subtract two digits from two digits with regrouping
- Make a two towers of ten (or draw them). Have a few ones as well.
    - Have your child figure out how to take away seventeen blocks, and ask them to explain what happened. How many tens and ones were there? How many tens and ones are there after you subtracted seventeen?
    - They had to take away one group of ten by subtracting the one ten in seventeen, and they had to take away a group of ten by breaking it into ones.
    (continued on the next page)

- Write the problem 73 – 29 vertically.
  - Ask your child if you can take 9 away from 3.
    - no
  - Ask your child where you can get more from so that you can subtract 9. (Hint: Think Legos or whatever you were just using.)
  - You are going to break up a stack of ten into ones. Those ten "blocks" are going to move from the tens column into the ones column because we need them there to take away the nine needed.
    - Cross off the seven. You are taking one away. Ask your child how many tens are left.
      - six
      - You took away a stack of ten. You broke it up into ones, so you can take away nine blocks.
    - Ask your child where the tens move to.
      - That ten is going to move to the ones column. Write a one next to the three. It's now thirteen. Three plus ten is thirteen. We didn't subtract anything yet. We just moved ten "blocks" from one place to another.
  - Now, you can take 9 away from 13. Ask your child the answer.
    - 4
  - There are 6 tens left and you are taking 2 away. What's the answer?
    - 4 tens, 4 ones, 44
- Lesson 16 worksheet
  - Part A: Have your child cross off the number of blocks being subtracted. They will have to cross off some from a group of ten which will turn the rest into ones.
  - Part B: Subtract with regrouping. Talk through the example 67 – 29.
    - Can you take nine away from seven?
      - no
    - What do you need to do?
      - Take a group of ten and move it to the ones.
    - Cross of the six and make it a five.
      - There were six groups of ten. Now there are five groups of ten. Where did the ten go?
    - Write a one next to the seven.
      - Now there are seventeen ones. How do you subtract now?
        - $17 - 9 = 8$
        - Write eight in the ones column.
      - Then subtract the tens. There are five tens with two being taken away.
        - $5 - 2 = 3$
    - The answer is three tens and two ones, 32.
    - You could watch your child do the first problem, but don't direct them. If they have a question, refer to the example about what the next step is.
  - Part C: Subtract. Some will need regrouping, some not.

Lesson 17
- Students will: solve two digit subtraction word problems
- Tell your child that Mark had four marbles and lost one of them. Ask how many he has now?
  - three
  - Ask your child how they figured out how many there are. How did they use four and one to get three?
    - They subtracted.
- Lesson 17 worksheet
  - Point out that the question they just answered is just like the first one on the page. Any time they don't know how to use the numbers in a word problem like these, they can just substitute little numbers to figure it out. (42 and 15 became 4 and 1 in the example.)
  - Some of the problems need regrouping and some don't.

Lesson 18
- Students will: solve one-digit word problems, determining whether to add or subtract
- Make a word story with you and your child. If the two of you ate ten _____, and you had eaten four of them, how many did your child eat?
  - If they aren't sure, encourage them to use a picture to figure it out.
  - $10 - 4 = 6$
- Make one more story problem. If you ate five _____, and your child ate seven more than you, how many did your child eat?
  - $5 + 7 = 12$
- Lesson 18 worksheet
  - They will have to think for themselves here and determine if they need to add or subtract to find the answer.
  - When you check, if they get any wrong, ask them if their answer makes sense, put the number into a sentence. (For instance, if he had more than Ethan, could he have only 4 cookies?)

Lesson 19
- Students will: solve double-digit word problems, determining whether to add or subtract
- The worksheet today will be similar to Lesson 18, just with bigger numbers. Remind your child that they can simplify the numbers if that helps them figure out if they need to add or subtract.
- Lesson 19 worksheet
  - When you check, if they get any wrong, ask them if their answer makes sense, put the number into a sentence. (For example, if some were broken, could there be more shells than what they started with?)

Lesson 20
- Students will: add and subtract
- Lesson 20 worksheet
    - They will add or subtract the number at the top of each rocket all the way down the numbers in the rocket.

Money

Lesson 21 (coins)
- Students will: use the fewest number of coins, calculate the value of coins up to one hundred cents, add and subtract ten from three digits, identify the value of a digit in a number, solve a word problem
- If you can, get out a handful of coins, making sure you have at least one of each: penny, nickel, dime, quarter.
    - Pretend your pencil is on sale for six cents. Ask your child how they could pay for it exactly.
        - one nickel and one penny
    - Ask what other coins they could use.
        - They could use a dime or a quarter.
        - On their worksheet they'll want to choose the lowest value coin for their answer.
    - Ask your child to make fifty cents using any combination of coins. They could try it different ways even.
    - Make sure your child can count the value of quarters: 25, 50, 75, 100.
- Ask your child what is 50 + 10.
    - 60
    - Now, ask what is 150 + 10, 250 + 10, 350 + 10.
- Ask your child what is 540 – 10.
    - If they aren't sure, ask what is 40 – 10.
- Lesson 21 worksheet
    - There are lots of parts to this worksheet. Remind your child to read the directions.
    - If your child chooses 25 cents for the first answer, ask what other coin would be closest to what was needed.

Lesson 22 (brown crayon)
- Students will: count the value of a group of coins, solve money word problems involving coins
- Lesson 22 worksheet
    - Part A: Count the value of the coins. Remind your child that it's easiest to start with the highest value coin. If you don't have a brown crayon or color pencil, they can just use their pencil to color in the penny.
    - Part B: Remind your child to use smaller numbers if they aren't sure what to do with the problems. Also remind them that their answer should make sense!

Lesson 23 (coins and one and five bills)
- Students will: add with regrouping, "buy" items with the least possible number of bills and coins, count by fives
- Get out fives, ones, and coins.
    - Have your child buy things in the room with exact change (or as close to it as you can get).
    - Have your child start with the highest value and work their way down in order to use the fewest bills and coins as possible.
        - For instance, if it was $3.64, you would start with the five dollar bill. That's too much. Then go to one dollar. You could use three ones. Another one would be too much. Then quarters, you could use two quarters. Then dimes, nickels, pennies…
- Lesson 23 worksheet
    - Part A: Pay for the items using exact change using the fewest number of bills and coins possible.
    - Part B: Count by fives starting at 13.
    - Part C: Addition – some will require regrouping. There are some written "upside" down with the one digit number on top. Your child can write a 0 next to the one digit number to remind them that there are no tens there to add.

Lesson 24
- Students will: problem solving and review
- Lesson 24 worksheet
    - Remind your child to read the directions carefully.

Lesson 25 (bills and coins, any value, brown crayon)
- Students will: count the value of bills and coins, subtract with regrouping
- Take out bills and coins and ask your child to count the value always using the next highest value of bill or coin.
- Have your child walk you through solving 25 – 8. Write it down and have your child tell you what to do next.
- Lesson 25 worksheet
    - Part A: Count the value of all the money.
    - Part B: Subtract. Some will require regrouping.

Lesson 26
- Students will: solve word problems involving money
- Lesson 26 worksheet
    - Remind your child to read the word problems carefully and to think about what they need to do to find the answer. Don't jump in. Let them think it over. If you need to help, help them make the problem simpler with smaller numbers or fewer toys, etc. to help them figure out how to find the answer.

Lesson 27 (a dollar bill, a dollar's worth of coins – Make sure to have pennies, nickels, dimes at least.)
- Students will: make change by counting on, divide shapes in half
- Ask your child how many more plates would you need to put on the table if there were four plates out and you needed ten.
  - After your child answers, demonstrating counting on to find the answer. Start with four and then count on 5, 6, 7, 8, 9, 10 while counting on your fingers.
  - You counted on six more.
  - That's how you'll be making change today because they haven't subtracted from "zero" before.
- Give your child a dollar bill and ask them to buy your pencil (or anything) for $0.42 cents.
  - You have to give change.
  - Start with 42 cents. Just say it out loud.
    - Now you can start with the smallest or largest coins, but I suggest starting with the smallest to make the numbers easier.
  - Put down three pennies, one at a time, and count 43, 44, 45.
  - Put down a nickel, and count 50.
  - Put down two quarters or five dimes and count on to 100.
  - The change (the answer on the worksheet) is the value of the coins you put down.
    - Have your child count their change.
- Lesson 27 worksheet
  - Part A: They will count on to make change. Let them use the coins.
  - Part B: They will divide the shapes in half. They don't have to be lines of symmetry.

Lesson 28
- Students will: subtract to find change from a dollar
- Ask your child how many cents are in a dollar.
  - 100
- You are going to complete a worksheet, but before you start, I want you to look at the first problem. You are going to subtract 20 from 100. We're going to do it together.
  - First you'll subtract the ones straight down. Zero minus zero is zero. You can write zero in the answer spot under the zeros in the ones column.
  - What's left? Draw a box around the 10 left in $\boxed{10}$0.
    - Now you have ten minus two left. You know the answer to that. What's ten minus two?
      - 8
      - Write 8 in the tens spot in the answer.
  - What's the answer?
    - 80
      (continued on the next page)

- Complete the worksheet. Each time draw a box around the ten in the problem. When you need to borrow more ones in order to subtract, you can cross off the ten and make it a nine. Then like normal you take those ten and move them into the ones column.
- Lesson 28 worksheet
  - They will subtract from one dollar by solving the word problems and using the amounts shown.

Lesson 29
- Students will: subtract money, solve money riddles
- Show your child their worksheet and have them read the amounts in the first two problems: 65 cents and 21 cents. Don't let them get flustered by the dollar signs and decimal points. You can put your finger on those and show them they are just subtracting normally.
- Next look at a problem where they are subtracting from $1.00. Let them know they can ignore the decimal point, the dot, and just subtract it like it says 100 cents. $1.00 is just another way of writing 100 cents.
- Lesson 29 worksheet
  - Part A: Subtract money vertically with dollar signs.
  - Part B: They will solve money riddles. Encourage them to test out each of the possible answers to see if it could fit.

Lesson 30
- Students will: add double digits with regrouping, recall addition facts
- Lesson 30 worksheet
  - Part A: They will just add vertically and regroup as necessary.
  - Part B: They are looking for facts in the puzzle. You can tell your child that they can have a high five and/or hug if they find any subtraction problems as well.

Rounding

Lesson 31
- Students will: estimate, make comparisons
- Teach your child that an estimation is a good guess about something. They are going to use estimation on their worksheet today.
- Lesson 31 worksheet
  - Part A: They are not to count the objects. They are to estimate, make a good guess, as to which box has more.
  - Part B: They are just to see the answer without measuring.
  - Part C: There are many answers to this. For the last column encourage them to think smart, not hard. (For instance, $30 - 30 = 0$ which is less than 25, of course.)

Lesson 32
- Students will: round to the nearest ten, solve money word problems
- Ask your child, if there were 19 people, would there be closer to ten or twenty people.
    - 20
    - That's called rounding. Twenty is a round number because it has a round 0 on the end of it.
    - Show your child the number line.

10 11 12 13 14 15 16 17 18 19 20

- Have your child find nineteen and see that it's closer to 20. Try it with other numbers. What's twelve closest to? What's fourteen closest to?
- Have your child show which numbers round down and which round up. You can tell them that five, since it's right in the middle, always rounds up.
- Lesson 32 worksheet
    - Part A: They are going to round. The closest round number that comes before and after each number is on the page. They just have to decide which way it goes.
    - Part B: Solve the money word problems.

Lesson 33 (ruler)
- Students will: practice rounding, adding and subtracting with regrouping, finding patterns, solving word problems, measuring inches
- Lesson 33 worksheet
    - Part A: They will decide if the number in the middle rounds up or down.
    - Part B: Show your child they can draw a box around 17 in the last problem.
    - Part C: They aren't solving these problems. They are finding the pattern. You could answer them orally and find the pattern in the answers if this is interesting to your child.
    - Part D: They will need a ruler to measure. And they will solve a word problem.

Lesson 34
- Students will: round to the nearest hundred, add to find the name values
- Go over rounding to the nearest hundred with your child. It's similar to tens. Work through an example to introduce it.
    - You're going to round 461 to the nearest hundred. Which number is in the hundreds spot?
        - 4
    - To round 461 to the nearest hundred we are asking, "Which is it closer to 400 or 500?"

(continued on the next page)

- We need to look at the number immediately to the right. Which number is to the right of 4 in 461?
  - 6
- Is six, 5 or more?
  - yes
- That means we need to round up. What's the next hundred after 4̲00?
  - 500
- Which is 461 closer to 400 or 500?
  - 500
- Try one more together at least. What is 129 closest to if you are rounding to the nearest hundred? It could round down to 100 or up to 200? What number do they need to check?
  - They need to check the digit next to the hundred, which is the two. Two is less than five, so they are going to round down to 100.
- Lesson 34 worksheet
  - Part A: Round to the nearest hundred by choosing between the options.
  - Part B: They are going to add the values of the letters. They can just add two numbers at a time and then add on the next value.

Lesson 35
- Students will: practice rounding to the nearest ten and hundred
- Lesson 35 worksheet
  - Part A: Round the numbers on the sides to the nearest ten.
  - Part B: Round to the nearest hundred.

Telling Time

Lesson 36
- Students will: tell time to the half hour
- Review reading a clock with your child. Have your child read the times on the clocks below.

- If they need reminders… The short hand is the hour. The hour is the number the hour hand has just passed (or is pointing directly at). Each number around the clock is five minutes. When the minute hand, the long one, is pointing to the six, that's thirty minutes.
- Lesson 36 worksheet
  - They need to write the times in digital format such as 1:00 and 4:30.

Lesson 37
- Students will: draw hands on clocks to the quarter hour, read and write numbers and money amounts, measure using a ruler, solve problems
- You can use the clocks from Lesson 36 to quickly see if your child remembers which is the hour hand and where it goes (after the hour), and what is the minute hand and where it goes (every number means five minutes have passed).
- Lesson 37 worksheet
  - Part A: They will draw hands on the clock.
  - Part B: They will write numbers they read.
  - Part C: They will write the dollar amounts they read.
  - Part D: They will determine the length using the ruler on the page. They just need to pay attention to do this because the ruler starts at 5.
  - Part E: Answer questions – pattern, hundreds and tens, figure out the problem.
    - If your child is confused with adding 5 hundreds and 3 hundreds, just have them use apples. What's 5 apples plus 3 apples? 8 apples So, 5 hundreds and 3 hundreds is 8 hundreds.

Lesson 38
- Students will: write times at five minute intervals, measure and compare lengths
- Have your child read these clocks.

- They need to think about the hour. The hour hand moves as time goes by. If it's almost the next hour, the hour hand will be closest to the next hour, not the hour it is right now. If it's shortly after the hour, the hour hand will be closest to the current hour. The minutes can be counted by fives around the clock, even if the numbers aren't there on the second clock. (Answers: 10:10 and 11:55)
- Lesson 38 worksheet
  - Part A: They will match the clocks to the times given.
  - Part B: Students will compare the number of units of the lengths of lines.

Lesson 39
- Students will: learn to tell time by words such as past and after, subtract, solve word problems
  - Ask your child what time they think five minutes after six would be.
    - 6:05
  - How about "half past four?" Here's a hint for your child: What is half way around the clock?
    - 4:30
  - Can they guess what "quarter past three" would be? What is a quarter of the way around the clock? Even have them divide the clock into four pieces.
    - 3:15

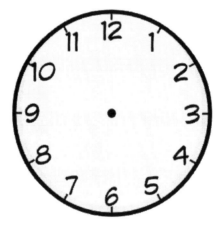

  - This is what they will be doing today for part of their worksheet. Finding the times that match the words. They will see the words past and after and need to find a time with that many minutes after the hour.
- Lesson 39 worksheet
  - Part A: Match the times and words.
  - Part B: Subtract.
  - Part C: Solve the word problems. There is an elapsed time problem. They are to find two hours later. The minutes won't change. If it's a struggle for your child. Have them draw the time on the clock here and then move the hour hand two numbers over.

Lesson 40
- Students will: practice known facts, match digital and analog times to time phrases
- Quiz your child on subtraction facts. Make sure your child is learning and retaining their addition and subtraction facts. We're going to be moving on to multiplication and division this year. They need to get their facts down. Use flashcards, our facts workbooks, or quizzing and games just five minutes a day to learn them and keep them up.
- Introduce another way to talk about time.
  - We can also say how many minutes there are until the next hour. We say it like this, "Five to eight." That means it is five minutes until eight.
    - Have your child draw five minutes to eight on this clock.
      - Remind your child that the hour is not eight yet. It's still five minutes before the hour hand will reach the eight exactly.
      - Can they tell it's almost eight by their clock?
        - It's 7:55.

- When we talk about time until the hour, we count by fives backwards. At the 11 there are just five minutes until the hour. At the 10 there are ten minutes until the hour.
- Have your child draw ten minutes to nine. It's not nine o'clock yet. There are still ten minutes before the hour hand reaches the nine.
  - 8:50
  - We can say this "ten to nine" or "ten of nine."
  - Ask your child what time it is on the first clock. Can they say it a different way?
    - five to eight
    - five of eight
- Have your child draw the time twenty of ten. They should count backwards by fives. The eleven is five minutes of ten. The ten is ten minutes to ten, etc.
  - 9:40
- Ask your child where the minute hand would be pointing at a quarter to three.
  - to the nine
    (continued on the next page)

- Lesson 40 worksheet
  - This is to cut out and play memory/concentration with time words, matching them to the times.

Lesson 41
- Students will: practice reading clocks, add with regrouping
- Lesson 41 worksheet
  - Part A: Match the clocks.
  - Part B: Add.

Lesson 42
- Students will: read clocks to the minute, subtract with regrouping
- Have your child count the minutes around the clock using the lines.
- Have your child read the time on the clock.
  - 10:11

The hour is the number the hour hand has passed. They can count by fives to get to ten and then one more to get to eleven, or they could count each individual line to get to eleven. (continued on the next page)

- Lesson 42 worksheet
  - Part A: Match the times.
  - Part B: Subtract with regrouping when necessary.

Lesson 43
- Students will: practice double digit addition, tell time to the minute
- Lesson 43 worksheet
  - Part A: Choose the correct time.
  - Part B: Add. Some require regrouping.

Lesson 44
- Students will: practice reading clocks to the minute, subtract with double digits
- Lesson 44 worksheet
  - Part A: Choose the correct time.
  - Part B: Subtract.

Lesson 45
- Students will: write times from time words, use Venn Diagrams to organize odd and even numbers and to compare numbers
- Lesson 45 worksheet
  - Go over the Venn diagram section with your child. Maybe start with the last one on the page. Choose a number. Is it odd? Is it less than 400? Which oval does it belong in?
    - If it doesn't belong anywhere, they write it outside the ovals.
    - If it belongs in both circles, then it goes in the space where they overlap.

Thousands

Lesson 46
- Students will: add to 20, use numbers up to 1000
- Write down the numbers 230 530 510 518.
  - Have your child compare the first two numbers. Which is bigger, 230 or 530?
    - 530
    - Five hundred is much bigger than two hundred.
  - Have your child compare, 530 and 510.
    - The hundreds are the same. So, they need to check the next biggest number, the tens.
    - 30 is bigger than 10 so 530 is greater than 510.
  - Have your child compare the last two, 510 and 518.
    - The hundreds and tens are the same, so they will have to compare the next biggest number, which is just the ones.
    - 8 is bigger than 0, so 518 is greater than 510.
    (continued on the next page)

- Lesson 46 worksheet
  - Part A: Identify numbers.
  - Part B: Compare numbers.
  - Part C: They will add (and subtract) to figure out the puzzle. The problems are all addition, but there are missing numbers. They could subtract or think, "What plus 3 equals 7?"
  - Make sure you keep working on addition and subtraction facts. They should know them and be quick at answering them. Use flashcards, our facts workbooks, and online games as ways to keep up the facts until they are superglued in their brains.

Lesson 47
- Students will: read and write numbers to the thousands, write numbers to the thousands in expanded form, practice subtraction up to 20
- Write the number 4173. Ask your child if they can read the number.
  - Ask your child how many thousands are in the number, then hundreds, then tens, then ones.
  - When they read it they are saying most of the answers, 4 thousand, 1 hundred, 70 is 7 tens, 3 ones.
- Lesson 47 worksheet
  - Part A: Write the numbers in expanded form by separating out the thousands, hundreds, tens, and ones.
  - Part B: Read the numbers and write them.
  - Part C: Solve the subtraction puzzles by following the arrows.

Lesson 48
- Students will: write numbers to ten thousands, compare numbers to the ten thousands, practice addition facts to 20.
- Write the number 23,415.
  - Read it together with your child.
    - They read the 23 and then say, "Thousand," when they get to the comma. Then they read 415.
- Have your child try one on their own, 51,260.
  - fifty-one thousand, two hundred sixty
- Just like we have ones, tens, and hundreds, we have thousands, ten thousands, and hundred thousands.
  - Ask your child which number is the ten thousands in the two numbers you wrote.
    - 2 and 5
    - twenty thousand and fifty thousand
- Ask your child which is bigger 29,999 or 51,111.
  - 51,111
  - It doesn't matter what the other numbers are. We compare starting at the biggest number.
  (continued on the next page)

- Lesson 48 worksheet
  o This is a good one to go over the worksheet with your child before they begin.
  o Part A: They are going to write the numbers described by the number of ten thousands, thousands, hundreds, etc. The first row has the numbers in order. The second line does not. They need to pay attention.
  o Part B: They need to write the biggest number. Encourage them to think about how they compare numbers, which digit do they look at first to compare numbers.
    ▪ To do this they will just write the next biggest number from left to right.
  o Part C: Add.

Adding Hundreds

Lesson 49 (scissors)
- Students will: use base ten blocks to add hundreds, add hundreds with regrouping, solve riddles
- Lesson 49 worksheet
  o Cut out the two pages of blocks, located on the following pages of the workbook.
    ▪ Save these in a plastic zip bag or something to be used again for subtraction.
  o Make these problems with the blocks. After working out each problem with the blocks, have your child solve it on the worksheet.
    ▪ Add 250 and 345.
      • Have your child make each number with the blocks and then combine the hundreds, tens, and ones.
      • Don't forget have your child solve it on paper.
      • 595
    ▪ Add 361 and 297.
      • This time when the tens are combined, there will be more than ten. You can regroup and trade ten in for a hundred. Do that and then count up for the answer.
        o 658
    ▪ Add 168 and 455.
      • This time the tens and ones will regroup.
      • 623
    ▪ Add 786 and 329.
      • This time every number regroups. Count by hundreds to figure out what ten hundreds equals. …800, 900, 1000. (continued on the next page)

- When you write this down, you can show your child how to write the one up next to the 7 but how there are no other thousands to add it to. One plus nothing is one, so they write 1 in the thousand place.
    - There's one final problem on the worksheet. Solve that without the blocks.

Lesson 50
- Students will: add hundreds with regrouping
- Lesson 50 worksheet
    - They will add hundreds. There are boxes to help them keep their place values straight and spots where they can "carry" the one.

Rounding and Estimation

Lesson 51
- Students will: round to the nearest ten, add hundreds with regrouping
- Lesson 51 worksheet
    - Part A: Round to the nearest ten.
    - Part B: Add hundreds.

Lesson 52
- Students will: round to the nearest hundred, add hundreds with regrouping
- Lesson 52 worksheet
    - Part A: Round to the nearest hundred.
    - Part B: Add hundreds.

Lesson 53
- Students will: find exact and estimated answers and compare them
- Lesson 53 worksheet
    - Use the worksheet, Part B, to show them what it means to estimate.
        - They will round each number to the nearest ten, and then they will add those numbers. The answer is the estimate, or good guess as to something close to the exact answer.
    - Part A: Add.
    - Part B: Estimate.
    - Part C: Compare the answers. This can just be yes or no.

Lesson 54
- Students will: find exact and estimated answers and compare them
- Lesson 54 worksheet
    - Part A: Subtract.
    - Part B: Estimate. (Just like the addition worksheet on Lesson 53.)
    - Part C: Compare.

Lesson 55
- Students will: estimate by rounding to the nearest ten, recognize times on analog clocks by their times written in words
- Lesson 55 worksheet
    - Part A: Round the numbers to the nearest ten and then add to find the estimation.
    - Part B: Match the clocks to the time words.

Lesson 56
- Students will: estimate and solve answers to addition problems, solve subtraction puzzles
- Write down the problem 24 – 3. Ask your child the answer.
    - Show your child how they only need to subtract the ones. Twenty minus no other tens is still twenty. 4 – 3 = 1 The answer is 21.
- Lesson 56 worksheet
    - Part A: They will solve the problems and then round to the nearest ten and then add those numbers together to find the estimate.
    - Part B: They will solve the subtraction puzzle.

Lesson 57
- Students will: practice adding the value of coins, estimate and solve subtraction problems
- Lesson 57 worksheet
    - Part A: They will solve the problems and then round to the nearest ten and then subtract the numbers.
    - Part B: Count up the value of the coins.

Lesson 58
- Students will: estimate and solve addition problems, review reading analog clocks to the minute
- Lesson 58 worksheet
    - Part A: Estimate and solve.
    - Part B: Write the digital times shown on the clocks.

Lesson 59
- Students will: estimate and solve subtraction problems, compare numbers
- Lesson 59 worksheet
    - Part A: Estimate and solve.
    - Part B: Compare the numbers and circle the greater number.

Lesson 60
- Students will: identify 3D shapes, write numbers from their representations
- Lesson 60 worksheet
    - Part A: Match the 3D shapes to their names.
    - Part B: Write the numbers based on the picture of thousands, hundreds, tens, and ones.

Subtracting Hundreds

Lesson 61
- Students will: subtract hundreds with regrouping using manipulatives
- Lesson 61 worksheet
  - Part A: Have your child use the base ten blocks (from Lesson 49) to build each problem. When they can't subtract what they need, they will have to regroup and trade in a ten for ten ones (for instance).
    - If you need more, they can be printed out from a link on Lesson 50 in the Math 3 course.
  - After solving each problem, they should solve it on the worksheet.
  - Part B: Solve the riddles.

Lesson 62
- Students will: subtract hundreds with regrouping
- Lesson 62 worksheet
  - Your child will subtract just like on Lesson 61 but without the blocks.
    - If your child is stuck and the blocks help, let them use the blocks.

Lesson 63
- Students will: subtract hundreds with regrouping
- Lesson 63 worksheet
  - They will just be subtracting in the same way.

Lesson 64
- Students will: subtract hundreds with regrouping
- Lesson 64 worksheet
  - They will just be subtracting in the same way.

Lesson 65
- Students will: identify number and shape patterns, compare numbers, use critical thinking to solve puzzles
- Lesson 65 worksheet
  - Part A: Identify and complete the number patterns shown.
  - Part B: Identify and complete the shape patterns shown.
  - Part C: Solve the number puzzles using what they know of comparing numbers and odd and even numbers.

Estimating Addition and Subtraction with Hundreds

Lesson 66
- Students will: round to the nearest hundred, estimate addition problems with hundreds
- Ask your child what 467 and 829 each round to if they are rounding to the nearest hundred.
  - They use the next number, the tens, to decide if it rounds up or down. They will round up if the tens place is five or greater. Otherwise the tens place rounds down.
- Lesson 66 worksheet
  - Part A: Round the numbers to the nearest hundred and draw a line to the answer.
  - Part B: Round each number to the nearest hundred and then add them to find the estimated answer.

Lesson 67
- Students will: estimate and add sums
- Lesson 67 worksheet
  - They will round the numbers to the nearest hundred and then add them to find the estimate. For the first four they will also solve the original problem.

Lesson 68
- Students will: estimate and find differences
- Lesson 68 worksheet
  - They will round the numbers to the nearest hundred and then subtract them to find the estimate. For the first four they will also solve the original problem.

Lesson 69
- Students will: estimate and add sums
- Lesson 69 worksheet
  - They will round the numbers to the nearest hundred and then add them to find the estimate. For the first four they will also solve the original problem.

Lesson 70
- Students will: estimate and find differences
- Lesson 70 worksheet
  - They will round the numbers to the nearest hundred and then subtract them to find the estimate. For the first four they will also solve the original problem.

Geometry

Lesson 71
- Students will: identify polygons, identify 2D shapes, identify numbers of sides and angles
- Lesson 71 worksheet
  - Part A: They will use the definition of a polygon to identify which shapes are polygons. If they ask you about one, have them compare it to the definition instead of telling them yes or no.
  - Part B: Match the polygons to their names.
  - Part C: Write the number of angles and sides each polygon has.
    - Show your child that the angle is the measure of the space between the lines, how far apart they are.
    - Ask them what they notice about their answers.
      - The number of angles and sides are the same.

Lesson 72 (a piece of paper you can fold)
- Students will: identify congruent shapes, identify lines of symmetry, draw symmetrical shapes
- Congruent shapes
  - Tell your child that congruent shapes are identical shapes. Ask your child if the covers of this parent book and of their workbook are congruent rectangles.
    - They should be.
  - Turn the one book sideways and ask if they are still congruent rectangles.
    - They are. The shapes are still the same.
    - On their worksheet they are going to look for congruent shapes.
- Lines of symmetry
  - Give your child the piece of paper and ask them to fold it in half so that the two halves line up perfectly.
    - Draw a line over the crease.
  - Ask your child if they can fold it in half another way.
    - Draw a line over the crease.
  - Ask your child if they can fold it perfectly any other way. The two halves have to line up as perfect mirror images when folded.
    - No, there are no more ways. (If it were a square, there would be two more lines, over the diagonals.)
  - The lines you drew are called lines of symmetry. They show the dividing line as to where the left and right or top and bottom sides are exact mirror images of each other.
  - On their worksheet they will be finding lines of symmetry. They can think of it as if the sides would line up perfectly when the shape was folded along that line.

  (continued on the next page)

- Lesson 72 worksheet
    - Part A: Find the congruent shapes.
    - Part B: Find the lines of symmetry. Draw a line where they could fold it in half and the two sides would be lined up on top of each other.
    - Part C: Draw the rest of the shape to make it symmetrical. They can just do their best. It's the thought that counts!

Lesson 73 (piece of paper you can cut up, scissors)
- Students will: identify congruent shapes, draw symmetric shapes
- Make sure your child remembers what congruent shapes are (identical, but can be shown in different ways, for instance one could be upside down).
- They are going to draw symmetric shapes today. There's a new word. On Lesson 72, they drew lines of symmetry. They are going to color in blocks to form symmetric shapes, shapes where each half is the mirror image of the other.
    - Take a piece of paper and fold it in half.
    - Have your child cut off some pieces.
    - Open it up and have your child find the line of symmetry.
    - Notice that the two sides aren't identical copies of each other. For instance, if the corner was cut off on the top right of the one side, it's the top left of the other side.
        - The sides are mirror images.
    - Try the first one of these on the worksheet together. They aren't copying what's in the right corner of the one side into the right corner of the other side. It would be in the left corner. They are mirror images, so that if you folded the paper in half, all the colored blocks would be right on top of each other.
- Lesson 73 worksheet
    - Part A: Find the congruent shapes.
    - Part B: Color in the blocks to make symmetric shapes.
        - Encourage your child to start at the line of symmetry and work out from there copying each row (blank, color, color...)

Lesson 74 (ruler, blocks)
- Students will: calculate the perimeter of regular and irregular polygons
- Perimeter
    - Tell your child that the perimeter is the measure around a shape.
    - Use a ruler to find the perimeter of their workbook. You can approximate lengths to the nearest centimeter or inch.
        - You will add the lengths of all four sides together to find the perimeter.
        (continued on the next page)

- Make any kind of shape out of blocks. Count around the sides of blocks along the outside of the shape to find the perimeter as measured in blocks.
  - Two blocks next to each other would have a perimeter of six.

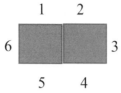

- Lesson 74 worksheet
  - Part A: Add to find the perimeter. When a side doesn't have a length written on it, then it is the same length as its opposite side or all the sides are the same length.
  - Part B: They are to count around the outside sides of the blocks to find the perimeter.

Lesson 75
- Students will: calculate the perimeter of irregular shapes, be assessed on geometry terms
- Lesson 75 worksheet
  - Part A: They will count around the outside of the shapes to find the perimeter.
  - Part B: Match the terms and definitions. If they ask you about a term such as congruent or symmetry, refer to the workbook page to show them congruent and symmetric shapes instead of telling them the answer.

Rounding and Estimation with Thousands

Lesson 76
- Students will: write numbers in the thousands in expanded form, round numbers to the nearest ten, hundred, and thousand, identify 3D shapes in everyday objects
- Rounding:
  - Write the number 2519 on a piece of paper for your child to see or use the workbook. It's the first problem in Part B.
  - Have your child help you write the number in expanded form by separating out the thousands, hundreds, tens, and ones.
    - $2000 + 500 + 10 + 9$
  - You are going to round to the nearest ten.
    - Have your child find the tens place.
      - The tens place is the one, so we're going to look at 19. Is that closer to 10 or 20?
      - 9 is not less than five, so it needs to round up to 20.
    - 2519 rounded to the nearest ten is 2520.
      (continued on the next page)

- Now, you are going to round to the nearest hundred.
    - Is 519 closer to 500 or 600?
        - You can use the next number on the right to help you decide.
            - One is less than five, so it rounds down to five hundred.
    - 2519 rounded to the nearest hundred is 2500.
- Now round to the nearest thousand. Find the thousands place and use the number next to it on the right to decide if stays the same or needs to round up.
    - 5 is not less than five, so two needs to round up.
    - 2519 rounded to the nearest thousand is 3000.
- On your 2519 you can circle the nine and draw an arrow to the one, circle the one and draw an arrow to the five, and circle the five and draw an arrow to the two. The next number to the right determines if it rounds up or down.
- Lesson 76 worksheet
    - Part A: Write the numbers in expanded form.
    - Part B: The first one you just did together.
        - If your child is stuck, underline the last two digits and round those to the nearest ten.
        - Underline the last three digits and round that to the nearest hundred.
        - Use the next number to the right, the hundred, to determine if the number rounds up or down in the thousands place.
    - Part C: Matching shapes to objects.

Lesson 77
- Students will: round to the nearest ten and hundred, practice subtraction facts
- Lesson 77 worksheet
    - Part A: Round to the nearest ten.
    - Part B: Round to the nearest hundred.
    - Part C: Follow the arrows to subtract.

Lesson 78
- Students will: estimate sums to the nearest thousand, practice addition facts
- Ask your child what five apples plus seven apples is.
    - 12 apples
- Ask your child what five thousand plus seven thousand is.
    - 12 thousand
- Lesson 78 worksheet
    - Part A: Find the estimated answer by rounding each number first to the nearest thousand.
    - Part B: Follow the directions to add.

Lesson 79
- Students will: estimate sums to the nearest thousand, practice subtraction facts
- Lesson 79 worksheet
    - Part A: Round the numbers to the nearest thousand and then add those numbers to find the estimated answer.
    - Part B: Match the subtraction problems to the answers.

Lesson 80
- Students will: estimate sums and differences
- Lesson 80 worksheet
    - Part A: They will need to round the numbers to the nearest ten, hundred, or thousand and add or subtract. They need to pay attention to the sign.
    - Part B: Add.

Lesson 81
- Students will: round to the nearest hundred and thousand to estimate sums, as well as find exact answers by adding thousands
- Lesson 81 worksheet
    - Part A: Round to the nearest hundred.
    - Part B: Round to the nearest thousand.
    - Part C: They need to find the exact answer to at least four problems.

Lesson 82
- Students will: round to the nearest hundred and thousand to estimate differences, as well as find exact answers by subtracting thousands
- Lesson 81 worksheet
    - Part A: Round to the nearest hundred.
    - Part B: Round to the nearest thousand.
    - Part C: They need to find the exact answer to at least four problems.

Lesson 83
- Students will: round to the nearest hundred and thousand to estimate sums, as well as find exact answers by adding thousands
- Lesson 81 worksheet
    - Part A: Round to the nearest hundred.
    - Part B: Round to the nearest thousand.
    - Part C: They need to find the exact answer to at least four problems.

Lesson 84
- Students will: round to the nearest hundred and thousand to estimate differences, as well as find exact answers by subtracting thousands
- Lesson 81 worksheet
    - Part A: Round to the nearest hundred.
    - Part B: Round to the nearest thousand.
    - Part C: They need to find the exact answer to at least four problems.

Lesson 85
- Students will: add one, tens, and hundreds
- Lesson 85 worksheet
    - They will add horizontally and vertically to fill in the blank boxes.

Lesson 86
- Students will: determine the elapsed time, practice addition

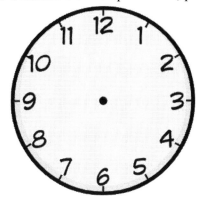

- Draw 1:15 on the clock.
    - Ask your child to count around the clock to see what time it would be two hours later.
        - 3:15
    - Then find out what time it is after three and a half hours.
        - Count on first the hours.
        - Count on 30 minutes, five at a time, moving from number to number.
            - 4:45
    - Then find out what time it is after two hours and fifteen minutes.
        - First count the hours and then the minutes.
            - 3:30
    - Then find out what time it is after 45 minutes.
        - Count around the minutes. The hour will change.
            - 2:00
- Lesson 86 worksheet
    - Part A: Find the elapsed time.
    - Part B: Follow the arrows to add the numbers.

Lesson 87
- Students will: find the elapsed time, practice subtraction
- Lesson 87 worksheet
    - Part A: Find the elapsed time.
    - Part B: Follow the arrows to subtract the numbers.

Lesson 88
- Students will: read analog clocks, write times, find the elapsed time, practice addition
- Lesson 88 worksheet
    - Part A: They will write the times and then find the elapsed time by counting around the clock, hours and then minutes, to get to the second time.
        - This is harder than the other worksheets.
    - Part B: They will follow the directions to add to fill in the blanks.

Lesson 89
- Students will: read analog clocks, write times, find the elapsed time, practice subtraction
- Lesson 89 worksheet
    - Part A: They will write the times and then find the elapsed time by counting around the clock, hours and then minutes, to get to the second time.
    - Part B: They will follow the arrows to subtract.

Lesson 90
- Students will: read a chart, solve word problems
- Lesson 90 worksheet
    - Part A: Use the information given to answer the questions.
    - Part B: Solve the word problems.
        - If they are ever stuck, have them try to figure it out with small numbers first.

Fractions

Lesson 91 (crayon optional)
- Students will: represent fractions with pictures, add and subtract double digits
- Lesson 91 worksheet
    - Part A: This is review, so I think it's easiest to just do it with the worksheet in front of you.
    - Have your child tell you which number in four fifths represents the number of pieces all together and which shows how many slices of pieces are left.
        - The bottom number shows the number of total slices in the pizza. The denominator tells the total number of pieces something is divided into.
        - The top number in the fraction shows the number of slices left. The numerator shows how many out of the total number.
    - Part B: Add to fill in the blanks.

Lesson 92 (piece of paper you can cut up, scissors, crayons are optional)
- Students will: find equivalent fractions, make representations of equivalent fractions, subtract double digit numbers
- Equivalent fractions:
  - Hold up your paper and tell your child you have one paper.
  - Cut it in half.
    - Ask your child how much paper you have now?
      - You have two pieces, but together you still have the same amount of paper.
      - You have two of two pieces and that's the same as one whole.
      - Hold up one of the pieces and ask how much you have?
        - You have one half.
  - Cut each piece in half again.
    - Ask your child how much you have now?
      - You have four pieces, but you still have the same amount of paper.
      - You have four of four pieces, and that's the same as one whole.
  - Take two of the four pieces and ask your child how much you have.
    - You have one half. These two pieces are equal to the one half you had before, even though there are two pieces now.
- Lesson 92 Worksheet
  - Part A: Color in and write equivalent fractions, fractions that are equal to the same amount.
    - Color in the first fraction to match the fraction shown.
    - Then color in the second fraction circle to match the first. The same amount should be colored in on both.
    - Then write in the numerator to show how many of the pieces are colored in.
  - Part B: Subtract to fill in the blanks.

Lesson 93
- Students will: write fractions shown by representations, add double digits
- Lesson 93 worksheet
  - Part A: Instead of parts of a circle, the denominator shows the total number of pictures, and the numerator shows the number of pictures that are shaded.
  - Part B: Add.

Lesson 94 (crayon optional)
- Students will: write and identify equivalent fractions by making representations of fractions using pictures, subtract double digits
- Lesson 94 worksheet
    - Part A: Color in the first picture according to the fraction written there. Then color in each box to look identical to the first. Write the number of pieces you colored in.
    - Part B: Subtract across and then down.

Lesson 95
- Students will: define geometry terms, determine the elapsed time
- Lesson 95 worksheet
    - Part A: Match the terms to their definitions.
    - Part B: They need to count on to find the number of hours and number of minutes that have passed. The minutes are to the half and quarter hour.

Lesson 96 (crayon optional)
- Students will: represent fractions with pictures, add triple digits
- Lesson 96 worksheet
    - Part A: They will color in the shape to show the fraction.
    - Part B: Add.

Lesson 97 (crayon optional)
- Students will: write and color representations of equivalent fractions, subtract triple digits
- Lesson 97 worksheet
    - Part A: Color in the first fraction picture to match the fraction given. Then color in the second the same amount to make them equivalent. Write in the numerator of the new fraction.
    - Part B: Subtract.

Lesson 98 (crayon optional)
- Students will: write and color representations of equivalent fractions, add triple digits
- Lesson 98 worksheet
    - Part A: Color in the first fraction picture to match the fraction given. Then color in the second the same amount to make them equivalent. Write in the numerator of the new fraction.
    - Part B: Add.

Lesson 99
- Students will: identify and write equivalent fractions, subtract triple digits
- Lesson 99 worksheet
    - Part A: Write in the missing numerator in the equivalent fraction. They can draw pictures or turn back to Lessons 98 and 97 for help.
    - Part B: Subtract.

Lesson 100 (crayon optional)
- Students will: define math terms, create symmetric shapes
- Lesson 100 worksheet
    o Parts A and B: Match the terms to the definitions.
    o Part C: Color in the blocks to make the shapes symmetrical.
        ▪ Remind your child that it needs to be a mirror image. If the paper were folded in the middle the colored blocks should be right on top of each other.

Lesson 101 (crayon optional)
- Students will: compare fractions, add double digits
- Lesson 101 worksheet
    o Part A: Comparing equivalent fractions
        ▪ Color in the fractions and use the pictures to determine which is greater.
        ▪ Make sure your child remembers which way to write the symbol, the big end points to the bigger number and the little end points to the littler number.
    o Part B: Add.

Lesson 102 (crayon optional)
- Students will: compare fractions, subtract double digits
- Lesson 102 worksheet
    o Part A: Comparing equivalent fractions
        ▪ Color in the fractions and use the pictures to determine which is greater.
        ▪ Make sure your child remembers which way to write the symbol, the big end points to the bigger number and the little end points to the littler number.
    o Part B: Subtract.

Lesson 103
- Students will: round numbers to the nearest hundred, compare fractions
- Lesson 103 worksheet
    o Part A: Compare the fractions. They can use the previous pages for help.
    o Part B: Match the numbers to what they are rounded to the nearest hundred.

Lesson 104
- Students will: compare fractions, round numbers to the nearest ten and hundred
- Lesson 104 worksheet
  - Part A: Compare the fractions as on the previous day.
  - Part B: Round the numbers to the nearest ten and nearest hundred.
    - You might want to have your child do the first row of rounding in front of you to make sure they are remembering how to do it.
      - They will use the next number to the right. To round to the nearest ten they will use the ones. To round to the nearest hundred they will use the tens.

Lesson 105
- Students will: estimate, round to the nearest ten, hundred, and thousand
- Lesson 105 worksheet
  - They will round the numbers to the highest place value. (If there are two digits, round to the nearest ten, three digits to the nearest hundred, four digits to the nearest thousand.)
  - Then they will add and subtract to find the estimation.

Multiplication

Lesson 106 (six little treats: chocolate chip, pretzel stick, etc.)
- Students will: be introduced to the concept of multiplication
- Introduce multiplication:
  - Multiplication is adding over and over again.
    - 5 times 2 is 5 + 5
    - 5 times 3 is 5 + 5 + 5
    - 5 times 4 is 5 + 5 + 5 + 5
      - That's like counting by fives 4 times.
  - If you put five books on each shelf and there were four shelves, you would have 5 + 5 + 5 + 5 books.
    - 5 x 4 = 20
  - Anything zero times is zero. A million times zero is zero.
    - Ask your child how much money would they have if you gave them a million dollars zero times.
      - zero, no money
  - Anything one time is itself. 8 times 1 is 8.
    - Ask your child how many pieces of candy they would have if you gave them one piece of candy eight times.
      - 8

(continued on the next page)

- 3 times 2 is the same as 2 times 3 (just like addition).
    - Ask your child to give you three chocolate chips (or whatever) two times. How many did they give you?
        - 6
    - Now you give your child two chocolate chips (or whatever) three times. Ask your child how many you gave them?
        - 6
- Lesson 106 worksheet
    - Part A: Do this together to show them how addition and multiplication are related and what a multiplication equation looks like.
    - Part B: They will write the multiplication equations. They can add or count to find the answers.
    - Parts C and D: They will use the Lesson 106+ worksheet to fill in the answers to the x 1 and x 0 and then 1 x and 0 x boxes.

Lesson 107
- Students will: illustrate repeated addition and multiplication problems to show the relationship, write multiplication problems from repeated addition problems, use the commutative property to find the answer to multiplication problems, learn the multiplication fact $2x2=4$
- Lesson 107 worksheet
    - I think this would be best to do together. Use the examples on the page.
        - They will draw pictures to show the problem.
        - They will write the multiplication problems.
        - Make sure they see that multiplication is just the fast way to do repeated addition.
        - Make sure they see that no matter which way you look at the problem you get the same answer. (ie. 2 x 3 = 6 and 3 x 2 = 6)
- Lesson 106+ worksheet
    - Learn 2 x 2 = 4 and fill it in on the chart.

Lesson 108
- Students will: multiply by ten and nine, learn the multiplication fact $2x3=6$
- Lesson 108 worksheet
    - I think this is one to do together to learn instead of doing a separate lesson.
    - Part A: Multiply by ten by adding zero.
        - You can go to the hundred chart on page 9 to see how any number times ten is that number with a zero on it. Skip count by twos and threes (starting at two and then three as the "one") and count to ten as you jump block to block and you'll land on twenty and thirty.
    - Part B: Multiply by nine with the trick. 9 x 5 = 45 5 – 1 = 4 and 4 +5 = 9
- Lesson 106+ worksheet
    - Learn 2 x 3 = 6 and fill it in on your chart (in two places, 3 x 2 = 6).

Lesson 109
- Students will: learn the multiplication fact 2 x 4 = 8, multiply using images and repeated addition, multiply by zero and one, calculate the value of coins
- Lesson 106+ worksheet
  - Learn 2 x 4 = 8.
  - Say it out loud. Say it both ways.
  - Ask your child 2 x 3, 2 x 2, 3 x 2, 2 x 4, and 4 x 2.
  - Fill it in on the worksheet in two places.
- Lesson 109 worksheet
  - Part A: Multiply by 1 and 0.
  - Part B: Use the pictures to write the problem and answer according to the example.
  - Part C: Add up the value of the coins.

Lesson 110
- Students will: learn the fact 2 x 5 = 10, multiply by 5, calculate with elapsed time
- Lesson 106+ worksheet
  - Add 2 x 5 and 5 x 2 on the worksheet.
  - Practice the facts you've learned so far.
- Lesson 110 worksheet
  - Part A: Go over the quick-trick rule on the page. There are lots of ways to do it though. They will eventually just learn and know the answers without having to think about it. Right now they can also count by fives to find the answer. Also, since 5 is half of 10, the answer of anything times five is half the answer of it times ten.
  - Part B: Find the elapsed time or find the new time after the given amount of time has elapsed. They need to count on to find the new time.

Multiplication and Division

Lesson 111 (scissors, glue, construction paper or file folder or other stiff paper)
- Students will: be introduced to division through seeing the connection with multiplication, learn the fact 2 x 6 = 12
- Lesson 106+ worksheet
  - Ask your child to figure out 2 x 6. That's six two times. If you gave your child six flowers, two times, how many would they have?
    - twelve
    - Have your child write in the answer for 6 x 2 and 2 x 6 on their worksheet.
    (continued on the next page)

- Lesson 111 worksheet
  - Cut the pieces out for your lapbook and glue them onto one side of your stiff paper. It doesn't matter too much how you do it. There's a title and there are two word problems. You can use the numbers to "write out" the equations to solve them. There are little holders that fold in half to form pockets to hold the numbers and equations on your page.
    - $2 \times 2 = 4$ and $4 \div 2 = 2$
  - They are to see the connection between multiplication and division.

Lesson 112 (scissors, glue, same stiff paper from Lesson 111)
- Students will: learn the fact $2 \times 7 = 14$, continue their introduction to division
- Lesson 106+ worksheet
  - Ask your child 2 x 7.
  - Have your child write in the answer twice on their facts square.
- Lesson 112 worksheet
  - There is another page of cutouts for the lapbook. Glue them onto the opposite side of the page or folder.
  - There's a heading and word problem. You can glue the kid pictures onto the page and as pockets.
    - Then you can solve the problem by literally dividing up the cakes between the children. How many go into each kid's picture pocket to give them all an equal amount.
    - You can also make up your own word problem and divide the cake up amongst yourselves, between toys, etc.

Lesson 113
- Students will: learn the fact $2 \times 8 = 16$, multiply and divide by two
- Lesson 106+ worksheet
  - Ask your child 2 x 8.
    - Have your child write the answer in both spots on their multiplication grid.
    - Quiz your child on the facts answered on their multiplication grid so far.
- Lesson 113 worksheet
  - They will multiply and divide by two. The important thing is seeing the connection with multiplication and understanding the concept of dividing into groups.

Lesson 114
- Students will: learn the fact $2 \times 9 = 18$, divide by 1, divide 0
- Lesson 106+ worksheet
  - Ask your child what is 2 x 9.
  - Have your child write in the answer in both places on the grid.
  (continued on the next page)

- Lesson 114 worksheet
  - Part A: Read through the top of the worksheet together with your child.
    - If you have 4 candies in one group, how many are in the group?
      - 4
      - If they aren't sure of the answer, give them four of something (books, pieces of paper, anything) and have them put them in a pile, one group. How many are there?
      - Write in the equation $4 \div 1 = 4$.
      - Ask your child what would be $10 \div 1$.
        - 10
      - Ask your child some other numbers. The answer is always the number. (eg. $100 \div 1 = 100$)
    - If you have 0 candies and divide them into 5 groups, how many are in each group?
      - 0
      - There are no candies!
      - If they aren't sure, give them a handful of nothing. Ask them to divide it up into 8 groups, 100 groups, any number of groups, it doesn't matter, it's always 0.
      - Write in the equation $0 \div 5 = 0$.
  - Part B: They will divide with 1 and 0 on their own.
  - Part C: They will multiply by two and add to find the perimeter. The perimeter is the measure around the shape. The opposite sides are equal length, so they can multiply it by two (double each number) and then add them together.

Lesson 115
- Students will: review multiplication facts, subtraction with regrouping, symmetry
- Ask your child if they remember what symmetry is.
  - Remind them that the line of symmetry is where you can fold a shape in half and the two sides will line up exactly.
- Lesson 115 worksheet
  - Part A: They should be able to quickly multiply by 0, 1, and 2.
  - Part B: They will subtract double digits. Some will require regrouping.
  - Part C: They will draw the line of symmetry.

Decimals

Lesson 116
- Students will: learn the fact 3 x 3 = 9, be introduced to the relationship between fractions and decimals, practice known multiplication and division facts
- Lesson 106+ worksheet
  - Ask your child to figure out 3 x 3. Multiplication is repeated addition. What's 3 + 3 + 3?
    - 9
  - Have your child fill in 9 as the answer on the 3 x 3 square on the chart.
  - Ask your child what 9 ÷ 3 is.
    - It's the opposite of multiplication.
      - 3
  - Ask your child what 8 ÷ 2 is.
    - 4
    - Show them how they can use their chart to find the answer.
      - They can find 8 in the column under 2 and then look across to find the answer, 4.
- Introduce decimals.
  - Decimals are a way of writing numbers. They've seen decimals before. $4.25 is 4 dollars and 25 cents. That dot is called a decimal point. It tells us that the number that comes after it are parts of 1. It's not 425 dollars. There are only 4 dollars. Then there are 25 parts of a dollar.
  - Ask your child how many cents are in a dollar?
    - 100
  - The decimal point tells us that 25 means 25 out of 100 cents, or 25 parts of a dollar.
- Lesson 116 worksheet
  - Look at the example together to see the connection between them in order to complete the worksheet.
  - They will fill in the decimal and money amount.
- Lesson 116+ worksheet – Do the first line on the worksheet.

Lesson 117
- Students will: learn the fact 3 x 4 = 12, write a decimal based on a visual representation, practice known multiplication and division facts
- Lesson 106+ worksheet
  - Ask your child to figure out 3 x 4.
  - Have your child write the answer, 12, into the two spots on the facts grid.
  - Ask your child 12 ÷ 3 and 12 ÷ 4.
    - 4, 3
  - Ask your child 9 ÷ 3.
    - 3
  - Ask your child other problems such as 10 ÷ 2 and 6 ÷ 1.
    (continued on the next page)

- Lesson 117 worksheet
  - There are 100 little blocks. They are to write how many are colored in as a decimal. If one line was colored in, that would be 10 out of 100 or 0.10.
- Lesson 116+ worksheet – Do the next line on the worksheet.

Lesson 118
- Students will: learn the fact 3 x 5 = 15, use decimals in writing monetary amounts, practice known multiplication and division facts
- Lesson 106+ worksheet
  - Ask your child 3 x 5. They can count by 5 three times to find the answer.
  - Have your child write 15 in the two appropriate grid squares.
  - Quiz your child on dividing. Use the answers they've filled in and divide them by the number at the top of the column or at the beginning of the row. The answer is the other number.
- Lesson 118 worksheet
  - They will write a dollar sign, then the number of dollars, then a decimal point, then the number of cents. At the top of the page either the dollars or the cents are zero.
- Lesson 116 + worksheet – Do the next line on the worksheet.

Lesson 119
- Students will: learn the fact 3 x 6 = 18, add decimals, practice known multiplication and division facts
- Lesson 106+ worksheet
  - Ask your child 3 x 6. They can add six three times to find the answer.
  - Have your child write 18 in the two appropriate grid squares.
  - Quiz your child on dividing. Use the answers they've filled in and divide them by the number at the top of the column or at the beginning of the row. The answer is the other number.
- Lesson 119 worksheet
  - They will add decimals today. It's exactly like adding regular numbers. They just need to remember to put the decimal point directly below in the same exact spot in the answer.
- Lesson 116+ worksheet – Do the next line on the worksheet.

Lesson 120
- Students will: practice multiplication and division facts, subtract decimals
- Lesson 106+ worksheet
  - Quiz your child on multiplication and division. Just use what's been filled in so far.
- Lesson 120 worksheet
  - Your child will subtract normally and then put in the decimal point in the answer directly under where it is in the problem.
- Lesson 116+ worksheet – Do the last line on the worksheet.

Lesson 121 (crayons optional)
- Students will: learn the fact 3 x 7 = 21, use money in word problems, make visual representations of fractions, practice known multiplication and division facts
- Lesson 106+ worksheet
  - Ask your child 3 x 7. They can add seven three times to find the answer.
  - Have your child write 21 in the two appropriate grid squares.
  - Quiz your child on dividing. Use the answers they've filled in and divide them by the number at the top of the column or at the beginning of the row. The answer is the other number.
- Lesson 121 worksheet
  - Part A: money word problems with cents
  - Part B: They will color in parts of the shape to show the fraction.
- Lesson 121+ worksheet – Do the first row of problems.

Lesson 122
- Students will: learn the fact 3 x 8 = 24, add money with dollars and cents, practice known multiplication and division facts
- Lesson 106+ worksheet
  - Ask your child 3 x 8. They can add eight three times to find the answer.
  - Have your child write 24 in the two appropriate grid squares.
  - Quiz your child on dividing. Use the answers they've filled in and divide them by the number at the top of the column or at the beginning of the row. The answer is the other number.
- Lesson 122 worksheet
  - Part A: They will add the money. This is just like adding with decimals, but they will need to remember to draw on the dollar sign.
  - Part B: They will solve the puzzle by figuring out the value of different coins added together.
- Lesson 121+ worksheet – Do the next line on the page.

Lesson 123
- Students will: learn the fact 3 x 9 = 27, solve money word problems, practice known multiplication and division facts
- Lesson 106+ worksheet
  - Ask your child 3 x 9. They can add nine three times to find the answer or use the multiply by nine trick.
  - Have your child write 27 in the two appropriate grid squares.
  - Quiz your child on dividing. Use the answers they've filled in and divide them by the number at the top of the column or at the beginning of the row. The answer is the other number.

  (continued on the next page)

- Lesson 123 worksheet
  - If your child is stuck on a word problem, remind them to make it simpler to help them figure it out. If it says $5.32, have them read it just five dollars while they are figuring out how to solve the problem. They could also draw a picture or even act it out to help them figure out what they need to do to find the answer.
- Lesson 121+ worksheet – Do the next line on the page.

Lesson 124
- Students will: practice known multiplication and division facts, add and subtract money with double digit dollars.
- Lesson 106+ worksheet
  - Quiz your child on dividing. Only use the answers that have been filled in.
- Lesson 124 worksheet
  - They will add and subtract. This is just like adding and subtracting decimals which is just like adding and subtracting normally. They just need to make sure they add the decimal point and dollar sign to their answer.
  - Remind your child to pay attention if they are supposed to add or subtract.
- Lesson 121+ worksheet – Do the next line on the page.

Lesson 125
- Students will: learn the fact 4 x 4 = 16, add and subtract money, practice known multiplication and division facts
- Lesson 106+ worksheet
  - Ask your child 4 x 4. They can add to find the answer.
  - Have your child write 16 in the two appropriate grid squares.
  - Quiz your child on dividing. Use the answers they've filled in and divide them by the number at the top of the column or at the beginning of the row. The answer is the other number.
- Lesson 125 worksheet
  - Your child will add and subtract. Make sure they pay attention to the sign.
- Lesson 121+ worksheet – Do the last line on the page.

Word Problems

Lesson 126
- Students will: learn the fact 4 x 5 = 20, solve addition and subtraction word problems including multiple steps, practice known multiplication and division facts
- Lesson 106+ worksheet
  - Ask your child 4 x 5. They can count by fives to find the answer.
  - Have your child write 20 in the two appropriate grid squares.
  - Quiz your child on multiplying and dividing. Use only what's been filled in on the chart.
  - If your child is stuck on a problem, try making up a story or rhyme about the answer or draw the equation and make it fancy or make the numbers into characters and hang it up.
- Lesson 126 worksheet
  - These are all word problems. Your child may need separate paper to write out their work. There are subtraction and addition problems, and some require both.
  - Remind your child to use simple numbers first if they are having a hard time figuring out what to do. For instance change 27 and 54 into 2 and 5 and figure it out that way first.
- Lesson 126+ worksheet - Do the first line on the worksheet.

Lesson 127
- Students will: learn the fact 4 x 6 = 24, solve addition and subtraction word problems including multiple steps, practice known multiplication and division facts
- Lesson 106+ worksheet
  - Ask your child 4 x 6. They can add four to the answer of four times five. Four times six is just four, one more time.
  - Have your child write 24 in the two appropriate grid squares.
  - Quiz your child on multiplying and dividing. Use only what's been filled in on the chart.
  - If your child is stuck on a problem, try making up a story or rhyme about the answer or draw the equation and make it fancy or make the numbers into characters and hang it up.
- Lesson 127 worksheet
  - These are all word problems. Your child may need separate paper to write out their work. There are subtraction and addition problems, and some require both.
  - If our child is stuck on how to begin a problem, remind your child to use simple numbers first. For instance change 45 and 78 into 4 and 7 and figure it out that way first.
- Lesson 126+ worksheet - Do the next line on the worksheet.

Lesson 128
- Students will: learn the fact 4 x 7 = 28, subtract money amounts, practice known multiplication and division facts
- Lesson 106+ worksheet
  - Ask your child 4 x 7. They can add four to the answer of 4 x 6 to find the answer. Four times seven is just four more.
  - Have your child write 28 in the two appropriate grid squares.
  - Quiz your child on multiplying and dividing. Use only what's been filled in on the chart.
  - If your child is stuck on a problem, try making up a story or rhyme about the answer or draw the equation and make it fancy or make the numbers into characters and hang it up.
- Lesson 128 worksheet
  - This is just a straight subtraction worksheet. Since they are subtracting money, every answer should have two decimal places (two digits after the decimal point).
- Lesson 126+ worksheet - Do the next line on the worksheet.

Lesson 129
- Students will: learn the fact 4 x 8 = 32, solve addition and subtraction word problems including multiple steps, practice known multiplication and division facts
- Lesson 106+ worksheet
  - Ask your child 4 x 8. They can double the answer of 4 x 4 to find the answer.
  - Have your child write 32 in the two appropriate grid squares.
  - Quiz your child on multiplying and dividing. Use only what's been filled in on the chart.
  - If your child is stuck on a problem, try making up a story, rhyme, or song about the answer or draw the equation and make it fancy or make the numbers into characters. Hang up your creation.
- Lesson 129 worksheet
  - These are all word problems. Your child may need separate paper to write out their work. There are subtraction and addition problems, and some require both.
  - If your child is stuck on how to begin a problem, remind your child to use simple numbers first. For instance change 28 and 63 into 2 and 6 and figure it out that way first.
- Lesson 126+ worksheet - Do the next line on the worksheet.

Review

Lesson 130
- Students will: learn the fact 4 x 9 = 36, add, estimate by rounding to the nearest ten, review math vocabulary, write digital times from time phrases
- Lesson 106+ worksheet
  - Ask your child 4 x 9. They can use a nine trick such as counting on their fingers to four, and then using the number of fingers on each side as the answer 3 and 6, 36.
  - Have your child write 36 in the two appropriate grid squares.
- Quiz your child on their vocabulary.
  - They don't need to know the exact definition, just the idea.
    - elapsed time – how much time has gone by
    - equivalent – the same, equal
    - symmetry – where the two sides are mirror images of each other
    - perimeter – the measure around an object
    - denominator – the bottom number of a fraction, the total number
    - numerator – the top number of a fraction, how much out of the total number
    - rounding – finding the closest easy number to work with
    - polygon – a closed shape with straight sides
- Lesson 130 worksheet
  - Part A: Add and estimate by using rounding.
  - Part B: They will read the time description (quarter of five) and write the digital time. They can look back to Lesson 41 if they need help.
- Lesson 126+ worksheet - Do the last line on the worksheet.

Lesson 131 (red and blue crayons)
- Students will: review multiplication, patterns, complete Venn diagram
- Lesson 131 worksheet
  - Part A: Color in or mark with the colors the numbers you say to count by two and to count by five.
    - Ask your child how skip counting is related to multiplication.
    - Every number colored in is an answer to a multiplication problem. Two, one time, is two. The first one colored in. Two, two times, is four.
    - If your child didn't know the answer, you can help them see it by asking these questions.
      - Two three times is what? Look at the third number colored in for two. What about five? What is 5 times four? (Skip count by five four times. Look at your chart.)
  - Part B: Venn Diagram
  - Parts C and D: Figure out the pattern. Encourage them to think, not just count to the answer. Can they figure out what it will be by skip counting maybe?
- Lesson 131+ worksheet – Do the first line on the page.

Lesson 132 (crayon optional)
- Students will: learn the fact 5 x 5 = 25, add, add in the hundreds with regrouping, find one half of objects, solve a word problem with multiple steps
- Lesson 106+ worksheet
  - Ask your child 5 x 5. They can count by fives to find the answer.
  - Have your child write 25 in the one appropriate grid square.
- Lesson 132 worksheet
  - Part A: Add.
  - Part B: They will color in half of the shape. Some are symmetrical; some are not.
  - Part C: Answer the word problem. They should draw a picture if they need help figuring it out.
- Lesson 131+ worksheet – Do the next line on the worksheet.

Lesson 133 (optional: coins 2 quarters, 4 dimes, 5 nickels and 7 pennies)
- Students will: learn the fact 5 x 6 = 30, use logic and knowledge of odd and even to complete a Venn diagram, review multiplication concepts, use coin values to add and find money amounts
- Lesson 106+ worksheet
  - Ask your child 5 x 6. They can count by fives to find the answer.
  - Have your child write 30 in the appropriate grid squares.
- Lesson 133 worksheet
  - Part A: They will count the dots to write two multiplication problems.
  - Part B: They will solve the addition money word problems. They will need to know the value of the coins. They may need another piece of paper to write down the amounts if they can't count the value in their head. They could also count the value using coins.
    - To solve the last one they could realize that 4 stickers is 2 stickers 2 times. The answer will be double the amount for two stickers.
  - Part C: They will fill in the Venn diagram. 67 will go outside of the ovals.
- Lesson 131+ worksheet – Do the next line on the worksheet.

Lesson 134
- Students will: learn the fact 5 x 7 = 35, use skip counting and multiplication to fill in charts, read a tally-mark chart to answer questions, use a price chart to answer questions
- Lesson 106+ worksheet
  - Ask your child 5 x 7. They can count by fives to find the answer.
  - Have your child write 35 in the appropriate grid squares.
- Lesson 134 worksheet
  - Part A: They can skip count and multiply to fill in the blanks.
    - For two treat bags, count by twos on your colored blocks. To find out how many peanuts count by twos twelve times. They would jump their finger along your chart and count twelve times.
    - Ten is easy. Just add a zero. What is 4 tens? 40. 12 tens is 120. (continued on the next page)

- o Part B: This is on the next page. They will count the tally marks to answer the questions. Make sure your child knows that a group with a diagonal line across it is five. They can count by fives to count up those.
    - o Part C: They will use the price chart to answer the word problems.
- Lesson 131+ worksheet – Do the next line on the worksheet.

Lesson 135
- Students will: learn the fact 5 x 8 = 40, skip count by three, add and subtract to fill in the missing numbers in subtraction equations
- Lesson 106+ worksheet
    - o Ask your child 5 x 8. They can count by fives to find the answer.
    - o Have your child write 40 in the appropriate grid squares.
- Lesson 135 worksheet
    - o Parts A and B: They will use subtraction, addition, and their thinking skills to fill in the blanks. If the problem is something like 45 - ? = 13 and they don't know what to do, have them think 4 - ? = 1 and then figure out how 4 – 1 gave them the answer so 45 – 13 will give them the answer.
    - o Part C: Count by threes.
        - ▪ Show your child that each number is an answer to a multiplication problem. Those numbers are 3 x 1, 3 x 2, 3 x 3, etc.
- Lesson 131+ worksheet – Do the last line on the worksheet.

Lesson 136
- Students will: learn the fact 5 x 9 = 45, skip count by four, create symmetrical objects, find missing numbers, problem solve, recognize odd and even numbers
- Lesson 106+ worksheet
    - o Ask your child 5 x 9. They can count by fives to find the answer or use a nine trick.
    - o Have your child write 45 in the appropriate grid squares.
- Lesson 136 worksheet
    - o Part A: They can do the opposite (subtract/add), count, guess use whatever technique they want to find what goes in the blank. Then they will just add.
    - o Part B: Solve the word problems. They can use pictures to help them figure out the answers.
    - o Part C: They will draw the other half of the object. A symmetrical object has two sides which are mirror images of each other. If you folded them in half, they would exactly line up. They should just do their best. They don't have measure the lengths of lines or anything.
    - o Part D: They will count by threes and fours. Each of those is an answer to a multiplication problem. Can you say some together? What's 24? 4 x 6, when you count by 4 six times
    - o Part E: Give your child some east-west and north-south highway numbers. You can use local roads. See if they can notice that the north-west highways are all odd numbered and the east-west highways are all even numbers. (continued on the next page)

- east-west: 66, 476, 238, etc.
- north-south: 95, 1, 405, etc.
- Lesson 136+ worksheet - Do the first line on the worksheet.

Lesson 137
- Students will: practice multiplication and division facts, solve addition and subtraction tables, count by tens with numbers that don't end in zero
- Lesson 106+
  - Use the page to quiz your child on multiplication and division facts. Only ask ones that you've done so far. Use the numbers along the top and bottom to multiply. You can reverse their order and ask both ways (eg. 4 x 8 and 8 x 4). Use the answer written in the grid divided by one of the numbers to the top or to the side.
- Lesson 137 worksheet
  - Part A: They will combine the numbers along the top and side either adding or subtracting. On the subtraction table they will subtract the smaller numbers along the top from the larger numbers along the side.
  - Part B: Count by tens starting at 3, so the first dot will be 13, then 23…
    - They can look back at the hundreds chart on page 9 if they need help seeing counting by tens starting at three.
- Lesson 136+ worksheet - Do the next line on the worksheet.

Lesson 138 (calculator-optional)
- Students will: learn fact 6 x 6 = 36, subtract from numbers with zero, order fractions with uncommon denominators, problem solve, practice facts
- Lesson 106+ worksheet
  - Ask your child 6 x 6. They can add six to 6 x 5 to find the answer. 6 x 6 is six just one more time. 30 + 6 = 36
  - Have your child write 36 in the appropriate grid square.
  - Quiz your child on multiplication and division facts. Encourage them to use what they do know to figure out the answer to what they don't know. They can multiply to divide, add to multiply, etc. The more they do it, the more automatic the answer will become. When they figure out an answer, you can have them repeat out loud the equation with the answer.
- Lesson 138 worksheet
  - Part A: Do the first one together. They are going to subtract (and one adding). When there is a zero in the first one, remind them to draw a box around the number. For instance, in 800, have them draw a box around 80 and then take away one from that. What's one less than 80, 79. Write 79 above it. So it's 10 – 5, 9 – 3, 7 – 1.
  - Part B: They just need to think about this. Each is the same number of parts. They can draw a picture if they need help figuring out that the bigger the denominator, the smaller the pieces, the smaller the fraction.
  - Part C: They will solve the word problems. They don't have to, but they can use a calculator on the last one.
- Lesson 136+ worksheet - Do the next line on the worksheet.

Lesson 139
- Students will: learn fact 6 x 7 = 42, add and subtract, compare fractions, compare values of a number of coins, problem solve, practice facts, count by fives
- Lesson 106+ worksheet
  - Ask your child 6 x 7. They can add six to 6 x 6 to find the answer. 6 x 7 is six just one more time. 36 + 6 = 42
  - Have your child write 42 in the appropriate grid squares.
  - Quiz your child on multiplication and division facts. Encourage them to use what they do know to figure out the answer to what they don't know. They can multiply to divide, add to multiply, etc. The more they do it, the more automatic the answer will become. When they figure out an answer, you can have them repeat out loud the equation with the answer.
- Lesson 139 worksheet
  - Part A: They will add and subtract. To find the missing number they can rewrite the problem as a subtraction problem. If they don't know what to do, have them try it with smaller numbers first, such as "What plus three equals four?" And ask how they got from 4 and 3 to the answer, one. You subtract four minus three. That's just what they'll do with the bigger numbers.
  - Part B: They could use real money if that helps.
  - Part C: They will use logic to compare the fractions. (This is just like on Lesson 138.)
  - Part D: Solve the word problems.
  - Part E: Count by fives to fill in the blanks.
- Lesson 136+ worksheet - Do the next line on the worksheet.

Lesson 140
- Students will: learn fact 6 x 8 = 48, subtract across zeros, practice facts
- Lesson 106+ worksheet
  - Ask your child 6 x 8. They can add six to 6 x 7 to find the answer. 6 x 8 is six just one more time. 42 + 6 = 48
  - Have your child write 48 in the appropriate grid squares.
  - Quiz your child on multiplication and division facts. Encourage them to use what they do know to figure out the answer to what they don't know. They can multiply to divide, add to multiply, etc. The more they do it, the more automatic the answer will become. When they figure out an answer, you can have them repeat out loud the equation with the answer.
- Lesson 140 worksheet
  - Solve the first one together. To subtract 500 – 244 you have to borrow or regroup. You can't take away four from zero. Ask your child what number they need to take away from to get ten more ones for the zero.
    - They will need to take one away from fifty. They can't take one away from zero.
    (continued on the next page)

- Draw a box around the fifty and ask your child what is one less than fifty.
  - 49
    - Write 49 above the 50.
- You now have ten to replace the zero in the ones.
- You can subtract from there.
  - 256
- Lesson 136+ worksheet - Do the last line on the worksheet.

Lesson 141 (crayon optional)
- Students will: learn fact 6 x 9 = 54, compare fractions, compare money amounts, write fraction and related decimal and money amount, practice facts
- Lesson 106+ worksheet
  - Ask your child 6 x 9. They can add six to 6 x 8 to find the answer. 6 x 9 is six just one more time. 48 + 6 = 54
  - Have your child write 54 in the appropriate grid squares.
  - Quiz your child on multiplication and division facts. Encourage them to use what they do know to figure out the answer to what they don't know. They can multiply to divide, add to multiply, etc. The more they do it, the more automatic the answer will become. When they figure out an answer, you can have them repeat out loud the equation with the answer.
- Lesson 141 worksheet
  - Part A: Count the value of the coins (and bills) and compare it to the money amount shown using the greater than/less than sign.
  - Part B: Color in five of the parts.
    - Ask your child to compare the two fractions. Which is greater?
    - They will use that knowledge to complete part C.
  - Part C: Compare the fractions.
  - Part D: They will write any fraction over 100 and then write it as a decimal and money amount with a dollar and cent sign.
- Lesson 141+ worksheet – Do the first line on the page.

Lesson 142 (brown crayon)
- Students will: compare the values of groups of coins, compare fractions and decimals, practice facts
- Introduce the term decimal places.
  - Write this fraction and decimal. 34/100 = 0.34
  - That is 34 hundredths. There are two decimal places (two digits) after the decimal point, so when you change it into a fraction you put it over 1 with two zeros.
  - Ask them to write their own number with two decimal places and to write it as a fraction.
  - If they do that okay (otherwise hold off), ask them to write a number with one decimal place. If they can't figure out what to do, show them again two decimal places. Underline the three and count, "One," and underline the four and count, "Two." (continued on the next page)

- If they are doing okay, ask them to try to figure out how to write that as a fraction. Reread the statement above, about two decimal places and two zeros.
- Here's an example. 0.3 and 3/10.
- Lesson 142 worksheet
  - Part A: Count up the value of the coins on each side and compare the totals. Make sure your child remembers which way the < > signs point.
  - Part B: Match the fractions to the decimals. When you check your child's work, point out the decimal places and ask how many there are.
- Lesson 141+ worksheet – Do the next line on the page.

Lesson 143 (brown crayon)
- Students will: learn the fact 7 x 7 = 49, compare the values of groups of coins, recognize tenths as decimals and fractions, practice facts.
- Lesson 106+ worksheet
  - Ask your child 7 x 7. Can they figure it out?
  - Have your child write 49 in the appropriate grid square.
  - Quiz your child on division facts. Encourage them to use what they do know to figure out the answer to what they don't know. They can multiply to divide, add to multiply, etc. The more they do it, the more automatic the answer will become. When they figure out an answer, you can have them repeat out loud the equation with the answer.
- Write for your child 1/10 and 0.1, one tenth. There is only <u>one decimal place</u> (one digit) after the decimal point, so when you change it into a fraction you put it over 1 with only <u>one zero</u>.
  - Have your child write their own tenth. They can choose any single-digit number to put after the decimal point and above the ten. 0.4 and 4/10 is four tenths.
- Lesson 143 worksheet
  - Part A: Count and compare the values of the groups of coins.
  - Part B: Match the decimals and fractions.
- Lesson 141+ worksheet – Do the next line on the page.

Lesson 144 (brown crayon)
- Students will: learn the fact 7 x 8 = 56, read fractions as numbers and words, write fractions, practice facts
- Lesson 106+ worksheet
  - Ask your child 7 x 8. Can they figure it out?
  - Have your child write 56 in the appropriate grid squares.
  - Quiz your child on division facts and some multiplication facts. Encourage them to use what they do know to figure out the answer to what they don't know. They can multiply to divide, add to multiply, etc. The more they do it, the more automatic the answer will become. When they figure out an answer, you can have them repeat out loud the equation with the answer. (continued on the next page)

- Write these numbers for your child to read.
  - Go over this reminder with your child. one decimal place, one zero; two decimal places, two zeros
    - .5 = 5/10   5 tenths
    - 0.68 = 68/100   68 hundredths
  - Then write .34 and 3/10 for your child to read the number and then write the matching decimal or fraction.
    - .34 = **34/100   34 hundredths**
    - **0.3** = 3/10   **3 tenths**
- Lesson 144 worksheet
  - Part A: Count and compare the values of the groups of coins.
  - Part B: Write the matching decimal or fraction.
- Lesson 141+ worksheet – Do the next line on the page.

Lesson 145 (crayon/s optional for coloring in grid)
- Students will: compare hundredths and tenths in decimal and fraction form, learn 7 x 9 = 63, practice facts
- Lesson 106+ worksheet
  - Ask your child 9 x 7. Can they figure it out?
  - Have your child write 63 in the appropriate grid squares.
  - Quiz your child on division facts and some multiplication facts. Encourage them to use what they do know to figure out the answer to what they don't know. They can multiply to divide, add to multiply, etc. The more they do it, the more automatic the answer will become. When they figure out an answer, you can have them repeat out loud the equation with the answer.
- Turn back to Lesson 141.
  - Ask your child which fraction is more five tenths or five hundredths.
    - Five tenths is bigger.
    - Ask your child why.
      - Each one of the five is a bigger piece.
      - Even one tenth is bigger than five hundredths.
- Lesson 145 worksheet
  - Part A: Have your child color in 3/10 and 78/100 on the page and write them as decimals, 0.3 and 0.78.
    - Ask which is more?
      - 78/100
      - Ask your child how many rows of ten are colored in on both.
        - 3 and 7 plus some
        - 7 is greater than 3.
        - They can compare the first digits first to see which is greater. They will compare the tenths first to see which has the most tens. That will be the greater number.
      (continued on the next page)

- - - Part B: Compare the fractions.
    - Have your child read some of them out loud.
  - Part C: Compare the decimals.
    - Have your child read some of them out loud.
- Lesson 141+ worksheet – Do the last line on the page.

Lesson 146
- Students will: practice multiplication and division facts, compare decimal tenths and hundredths, add with regrouping
- Use the 106+ worksheet to quiz your child on division facts. Start with an answer that's been filled in. Ask for it divided by the number at the beginning of the column or row.
- Ask your child to write the decimals five tenths and twenty-four hundredths and to tell you which is greater and why?
  - 0.5 and 0.24
  - Five tenths is greater because the other only has two tenths.
- Lesson 146 worksheet
  - Part A: Compare the decimals. If they are getting lost, you can go back to Lesson 145 and look at the decimals and the grids colored in. You could also have your child underline the tenths in each number (the first one after the decimal point).
  - Part B: Add.
- Lesson 146+ worksheet – Do the first line on the page.

Lesson 147
- Students will: learn the fact 8 x 8 = 64, practice multiplication and division facts, compare fractions to decimals, subtract with regrouping
- Lesson 106+ worksheet
  - Ask your child 8 x 8. Can they figure it out?
  - Have your child write 64 in the appropriate grid square.
    - What patterns do they see on the grid?
  - Quiz your child on some division facts and a few multiplication facts.
- Lesson 147 worksheet
  - Part A: Have your child read out loud the numbers across the top of the page: two tenths, eight tenths, nine tenths, seven tenths. They will compare them just by seeing them that way: two tenths is less than eight tenths because two is less than eight. It doesn't matter what form the number is written in.
  - Part B: Subtract.
- Lesson 146+ worksheet – Do the next line on the page.

Lesson 148
- Students will: learn the fact 8 x 9, practice multiplication and division facts, add hundreds with regrouping, identify fractions as decimals and decimals as fractions.
- Lesson 106+ worksheet
  - Ask your child 8 x 9. Can they figure it out?
  - Have your child write 72 in the appropriate grid squares.
  - Quiz your child on division facts.
- Lesson 148 worksheet
  - Part A: Match the fractions and decimals.
  - Part B: Add.
- Lesson 146+ worksheet – Do the next line on the page.

Lesson 149
- Students will: learn the fact 9 x 9 = 81, practice facts, subtract three-digit numbers with regrouping, write hundredths values shown by visual representations of the numbers
- Lesson 106+ worksheet
  - Ask your child 9 x 9. Can they figure it out?
  - Have your child write 81 in the appropriate grid square.
  - Quiz your child on facts.
  - Celebrate learning the last fact!
- Turn to Lesson 148's worksheet and have your child read down the first column of decimals.
  - twelve hundredths, two tenths, two hundredths, twenty-two hundredths
- Lesson 149 worksheet
  - Part A: Write the decimal value. Encourage them to count each column by tens!
  - Part B: Subtract.
- Lesson 146+ worksheet – Do the next line on the worksheet.

Lesson 150
- Students will: use place value to identify numbers, make change from bills, practice facts
- Look at the worksheet together before they start.
- Lesson 150 worksheet
  - Part A: Have your child identify the tens, ones, tenths, and hundredths in the first number.
    - 3 tens, 1 one, 6 tenths, 4 hundredths
  - Part B: They should write out the subtraction problems. They can ignore the decimal if it bothers them. They will put a box around the 1.0 just like it was a ten and then take one away and make it nine. The same thing goes with subtracting from ten dollars and one hundred dollars. They will put a box around 10.0 and take one away to get 99 and put a box around 100.0 and take one away to get 999.
- Lesson 146+ worksheet – Do the last line on the page.

Measurement

Lesson 151
- Students will: measure to the sixteenth inch, practice multiplication facts
- Use the Lesson 151 worksheet to show your child how to read the inch ruler.
    - Have your child count the number of lines that make up one inch. When they get to 16, they are at the next inch, that's 16 out of 16 parts, or 1, one inch.
    - Have your child find where half an inch would be.
        - Right in the middle, 8 out of 16, or ½.
    - Have your child find where a quarter of an inch could be. That's one inch divided into four parts. There are extra-long lines showing each quarter.
        - That's 4 out of 16 parts or ¼.
- Lesson 151 worksheet
    - Part A: Multiply.
    - Part B: Read the first ruler to see where the first mark is pointing and then find that number above it to match.

Lesson 152
- Students will: write multiplication and division fact families, measure to the millimeter
- Use the worksheet to show your child how to read a centimeter ruler.
    - Have your child count the number of lines that make up a centimeter.
        - When they get to ten, that's ten out of ten, or one centimeter.
        - Each line is one millimeter, or one tenth. If they count over 4 lines, that's four tenths.
- Lesson 152 worksheet
    - Part A: They will fill in the blanks in Part A by using the example and what they know about fact families. Multiplication and division are the opposite just like addition and subtraction are opposite operations.
    - Part B: They will read the centimeter ruler. This is like Lesson 151.

Lesson 153 (ruler)
- Students will: practice facts, solve money word problems, measure objects to the nearest millimeter and sixteenth inch
- Your child should be working on facts each day. You can quiz, use a workbook, use online programs like Xtra Math, etc.
- Lesson 153 worksheet
    - Part A: They will use the prices to figure out the answers.
    - Part B: This is on the next page. They will measure things in your house: books, drawer, tissue box, etc. They will record each measurement in inches and in centimeters.
        - If your ruler only has one or the other, you can print a ruler from online, or just use what you have.
        (continued on the next page)

- They can just measure to the nearest millimeter or sixteenth of an inch (meaning to the closest little line on the ruler).
- The centimeters they will write with a decimal. The inches they will write with a fraction.
- They can refer back to Lessons 151 and 152 if they need help remembering how to write the measurement.

Lesson 154 (dice, scissors)
- Students will: calculate the perimeter of a rectangle given the length of two sides, convert grams to kilograms and kilograms to grams
- Converting kilograms to grams and grams to kilograms.
  - Cut the Lesson 154 workbook page, Part A, to get ten pieces of paper labeled 100 grams.
  - Show your child that one of those papers is one tenth of the whole kilogram.
  - Hold up two papers and ask how many grams and how many kilograms.
    - 200 grams, 0.2 kilograms (two tenths)
    - Try some more and make sure they see the pattern.
      - 300 grams, 0.3 kilograms, etc.
- Lesson 154 worksheet
  - Part B: Find the perimeter.
    - Have your child roll the dice twice and record those numbers as the width and length of the rectangle.
    - Then they will figure out the perimeter, the measure around the outside of a shape.
      - Have your child draw a picture of a rectangle and label the measure of each side if they don't know how to get started.
  - Part C: Match the gram and kilogram amounts.

Lesson 155
- Students will: review time words, solve word problems with decimals, review math vocabulary
- Lesson 155 worksheet
  - Part A: Match the times.
  - Part B: They will use Lesson 100 to review vocabulary.
  - Part C: Solve the word problems using the numbers in the chart.

Lesson 156
- Students will: review fractions, solve word problems with decimals
- Lesson 156 worksheet
  - Part A: Color in the shape to show the fraction.
  - Part B: Solve the word problems using the numbers in the chart.

Review

Lesson 157
- Students will: read a scale to the 16th mark, use a tally-mark chart to answer the questions
- Lesson 157 worksheet
  - o Part A: They will count the tally marks and use the info to answer the questions.
  - o Part B: The scale is like a ruler. Weight in America is measured in pounds and ounces. There are 16 ounces in a pound, just like there are 16 parts to an inch.

Lesson 158
- Students will: estimate weights, multiply
- Pick up some things and ask you child if they weigh closer to 1 ounce, 1 pound, 10 pounds, or 100 pounds.
  - o This is just an estimation.
- Lesson 158 worksheet
  - o Part A: Estimate weights.
  - o Part B: Multiply by three and five. Use the hundreds chart to count by twelves.

Lesson 159 (teaspoon, tablespoon, cup, gallon jug if you can)
- Students will: solve problems
- Lesson 159 worksheet
  - o Part A: Add, multiply, subtract. Fill in the blanks.
  - o Part B: Solve word problems.
  - o Part C: Check the conversions to see if they are correct. Measure teaspoons into tablespoons, tablespoons into cups, etc.

Lesson 160
- Students will: solve problems
- Liters are used to measure liquids. There are one thousand millimeters in a liter like there are 1000 grams in a kilogram.
- Lesson 160 worksheet
  - o Part A: Add, subtract, multiply. Fill in the blanks.
  - o Part B: Solve word problems.
  - o Part C: Match the measurements.

Lesson 161
- Students will: solve word problems
- Lesson 161 worksheet

Lesson 162
- Students will: solve word problems
- Lesson 162 worksheet

Lesson 163
- Students will: estimate answers, solve number riddle
- Lesson 163 worksheet
  - Part A: They will round the numbers to the nearest ten and hundred and then add to find the estimated answer.
  - Part B: They will solve the riddle using the clues.

Lesson 164
- Students will: solve word problems
- Lesson 164 worksheet

Lesson 165
- Students will: solve word problems
- Lesson 165 worksheet

Lesson 166
- Students will: solve word problems
- Lesson 166 worksheet

Lesson 167
- Students will: solve word problems
- Lesson 167 worksheet

Lesson 168
- Students will: solve word problems
- Lesson 168 worksheet

Lesson 169
- Students will: solve word problems
- Lesson 169 worksheet

Lesson 170
- Students will: calculate perimeter, find equivalent fractions, draw symmetrical objects
- Lesson 170 worksheet
  - Part A: They will add the measures of the four sides to find the perimeter.
  - Part B: Find the equivalent fractions.
  - Part C: Draw the rest of the symmetrical object.

Graphs

Lesson 171
- Students will: read bars graphs to answer questions
- Turn to the worksheet with your child and go over the graphs. Find the titles, the vertical and horizontal axis labels that tell what the numbers show along the side and bottom. Read what some of the bars means.
- Lesson 171 worksheet
    - Part A: They will answer the questions by using the first graph.
    - Part B: They will answer the questions by using the second graph. Your child will need to know the word horizontal. The horizontal axis runs across the bottom.

Lesson 172 (crayons: optional)
- Students will: create a bar graph and use the graph to answer questions
- Lesson 172 worksheet
    - They will color in one block on the graph for each tally mark. When they are finished, they will use the graph to answer the questions.

Lesson 173 (crayons/colored pencils – five colors)
- Students will: create a circle graph and use it to answer questions
- Show your child the worksheet page. They will be making a circle graph, also called a pie chart.
- Lesson 173 worksheet
    - They need to color in each square by the labels, each a different color.
    - Then they will color in the number of pieces shown by the tally marks with the matching color.
    - Finally they will use the graph to answer the questions.

Lesson 174 (crayons/colored pencils – eight colors)
- Students will: create a circle graph
- Ask your child how many hours are in a day.
    - 24 hours
    - Their worksheet is about how they spend their time in one day, so it is divided into 24 pieces.
- Lesson 174 worksheet
    - They will fill in the chart with estimates of how they use their time.
    - Then they will color in the boxes next to the labels, each a different color.
    - Then they will color in the number of pieces based on the numbers they wrote.

Lesson 175
- Students will: read a line graph to answer questions
- Show your child the line graph on their worksheet. Find the title, the horizontal axis, vertical axis, and number labels. Instead of bars, there is a dot to show the number for each one.
- Lesson 175 worksheet
    - They will use the graph to answer the questions.

Lesson 176
- Students will: read the pictograph to answer the question
- Go to the worksheet for Lesson 176 and look at the pictograph. Have your child find the title and the key. The key shows how many books each picture represents.
    - Ask your child to read the key and see how many books is represented by each picture of a book.
        - In this graph each book is four books.
    - Have your child figure out how many books two books would represent.
        - 8 books
    - Last one, your child needs to understand what a picture of a half of a book represents.
        - 2 books
- Lesson 176 worksheet
    - They will use the pictograph to answer the questions.

Lesson 177
- Students will: use the pictograph to answer the questions
- Lesson 177 worksheet

Lesson 178 (two dice, two crayons)
- Students will: multiply
- Lesson 178 worksheet
    - This is an easy multiplication game. They will multiply the two numbers on the dice and mark the answer with their color.
    - You can play too and color in answers in another color, or your child can play until they get five in a row.

Lesson 179
- Students will: divide
- Lesson 179 worksheet
    - They will complete the division squares by dividing across and down.

Lesson 180 (die, two game pieces of some sort like coins)
- Students will: multiply and divide
- Lesson 180 worksheet
    - Roll the die. Move the number of spaces and answer the problem.
    - First to the end wins.
- Celebrate! You've finished Math 3!

EP Math 3

Workbook Answers

Lesson 1

100s Chart, Comparison & 2D Shapes

A. Fill in the missing numbers on the 100s chart puzzles.

17	18			34	35		68	69	70
27	28	29		43	44	45	77	78	79	80
	38	39		53	54			88	89

B. Compare the numbers using <, >, or =.

54 > 45   42 < 68   35 > 16 + 15
28 < 29   55 < 81   56 = 47 + 9
72 = 72   60 > 49   62 > 56 + 5

C. Draw the shape in each box according to the given name.

Circle   Oval   Triangle   Square   Diamond

Rectangle   Pentagon   Hexagon   Octagon   Star

Lesson 2

Adding to 20 & Tens and Ones

A. Make the scales balance by filling in the correct numbers.

3 + 5   8   =   2 + 7   9   =
4 + 6   10   =   4 + 8   12   =
6 + 9   15   =   7 + 9   16   =

B. Count the number of blocks in each set. Write the numbers.

15   33   47
50   82

Lesson 3

Money, Measurement & Telling Time

A. Color all the pennies brown. Count the coins and write the amount in cents.

3 ¢   30 ¢   22 ¢
20 ¢   31 ¢   75 ¢

B. Use your ruler to measure the length of the path in inches.

7 in

C. Write the time underneath each clock.

10:00   7:15   2:30   12:45

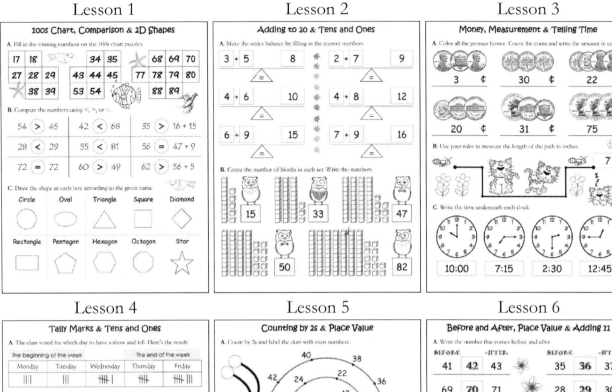

Lesson 4

Tally Marks & Tens and Ones

A. The class voted for which day to have a show and tell. Here's the result:

The beginning of the week			The end of the week	
Monday	Tuesday	Wednesday	Thursday	Friday
|||	|||	‖‖		‖‖	‖‖ |||

1. Which day had the most votes? Friday
2. Which day had the fewest votes? Tuesday
3. How many votes altogether? 26
4. How many votes for the end of the week? 13
5. How many votes for the beginning of the week? 7

B. Count the number of blocks in each set. Write the numbers.

14   32   48
43   85

Lesson 5

Counting by 2s & Place Value

A. Count by 2s and label the dots with even numbers.

40 38 42 24 22 36 14 12 26 6 4 20 2 10 34 44 28 8 18 46 16 30 32

B. Make numbers using hundreds, tens, and ones. Match the same numbers.

400 30 8   ●   ● 953
50 900 3   ●   ● 335
700 2 30   ●   ● 438
5 80 300   ●   ● 732

Lesson 6

Before and After, Place Value & Adding 11

A. Write the number that comes before and after.

BEFORE	AFTER		BEFORE	AFTER
41	42	43	35	36	37
69	70	71	28	29	30

B. Write a number that matches the place value description.

7 is in the tens place: 2 is in the ones place: 1 is in the hundreds place:

Answers will vary.

C. Add 11. Fill in the missing numbers on the 100s chart puzzles.

22		64		89		35	36
	33		75		100		46	47
17		45		91		70	71
	28		56		102		81	82
56		39		27		83	84
	67		50		38		94	95

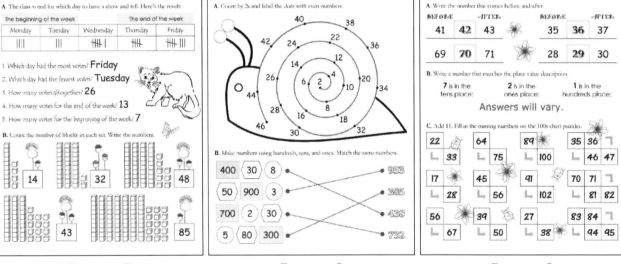

Lesson 7

Counting by 10s & Adding Tens

A. Count the number of blocks. Fill in the blanks.

35 + 10 = 45   43 + 30 = 73

B. Count by 10s. Fill in the missing numbers.

3 13 23 ✗ 63 73 83
33 43 53 ✗ 93
+10

C. Solve the addition problems.

| 75 +10 = 85 | 33 +10 = 43 | 68 +10 = 78 |
| 10 +56 = 66 | 10 +19 = 29 | 10 +10 = 20 |

| 46 +10 = 56 | 62 +10 = 72 | 46 +20 = 66 |
| 37 +20 = 57 | 51 +30 = 81 | 40 +13 = 53 |

Lesson 8

Adding 1-Digit with Regrouping

A. Count the number of blocks. Fill in the blanks.

38 + 5 = 43   49 + 7 = 56

B. Let's practice addition with regrouping. The first one is done for you.

| 24 +8 = 32 | 35 +9 = 44 | 19 +8 = 27 | 57 +6 = 63 | 76 +9 = 85 | 48 +3 = 51 |

C. Solve the addition problems. Some of the problems may need regrouping.

| 46 +5 = 51 | 57 +8 = 65 | 64 +3 = 67 |
| 32 +6 = 38 | 18 +6 = 24 | 78 +5 = 83 |

| 65 +2 = 67 | 16 +6 = 22 | 85 +7 = 92 |
| 29 +7 = 36 | 43 +5 = 48 | 31 +9 = 40 |

Lesson 9

Adding 2-Digits with Regrouping

A. Count the number of blocks. Fill in the blanks.

27 + 18 = 45   25 + 37 = 62

B. Let's practice addition with regrouping. The first one is done for you.

| 25 +38 = 63 | 57 +24 = 81 | 26 +49 = 75 |
| 34 +19 = 53 | 32 +48 = 80 | 78 +26 = 104 |

B. Solve the addition problems. Some of the problems may need regrouping.

| 59 +83 = 142 | 74 +52 = 126 | 49 +75 = 124 |
| 23 +74 = 97 | 68 +34 = 102 | 20 +35 = 55 |

| 17 +92 = 109 | 74 +94 = 168 | 28 +68 = 96 |
| 54 +58 = 112 | 37 +86 = 123 | 58 +42 = 100 |

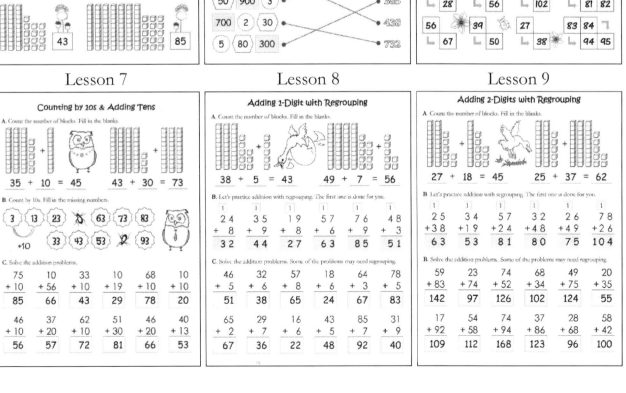

Lesson 10

Addition Word Problems

Solve each word problem. Write the equation and the answer.

Mark has thirteen books. Sam has twenty-six books. How many books do they have in total?
13 + 26 = 39
39 books

Bill has 42 marbles. Ethan gave Bill 36 marbles. How many marbles does Bill have now?
42 + 36 = 78
78 marbles

Owen found 16 ladybugs in the yard. Grace found 17 ladybugs. How many ladybugs did they find together?
16 + 17 = 33
33 ladybugs

Emma had twenty-eight dimes. Her mom gave her fifteen more dimes. How many dimes does Emma have now?
28 + 15 = 43
43 dimes

Larry read 37 pages of his storybook yesterday. He read 24 pages today. How many pages did Larry read in all?
37 + 24 = 61
61 pages

Jenny picked 28 apples from the apple tree. Noah picked 39 apples. How many apples did they pick in total?
28 + 39 = 67
67 apples

There were thirty-four books on the shelf. Orson placed sixteen more books. How many books are there now on the shelf?
34 + 16 = 50
50 books

At the garden, Henry planted 35 flowers. Olivia planted 25 flowers. How many flowers did they plant in total?
35 + 25 = 60
60 flowers

Lesson 11

Counting Back by 10s & Subtracting Tens

A. Count the number of blocks. Fill in the blanks.

35 - 10 = 25   63 - 10 = 53

B. Count back by 10s. Fill in the missing numbers.

90 80 70 __ 30 20 10
-10   60 50 40

C. Solve the subtraction problems.

70	10	16	64	55	21
- 10	- 10	- 10	- 10	- 10	- 10
60	0	6	54	45	11

83	29	48	97	35	76
- 10	- 10	- 10	- 10	- 10	- 10
73	19	38	87	25	66

Lesson 12

Subtracting 1-Digit without Regrouping

A. Count the number of blocks. Fill in the blanks.

38 - 5 = 33   49 - 7 = 42

B. Solve the subtraction problems.

58	19	68	19	47	36
- 7	- 4	- 2	- 3	- 1	- 4
51	15	66	16	46	32

57	78	39	65	29	78
- 4	- 5	- 9	- 3	- 2	- 6
53	73	30	62	27	72

29	47	98	87	28	13
- 6	- 2	- 4	- 3	- 0	- 3
23	45	94	84	28	10

Lesson 13

Subtracting 2-Digits without Regrouping

A. Count the number of blocks. Fill in the blanks.

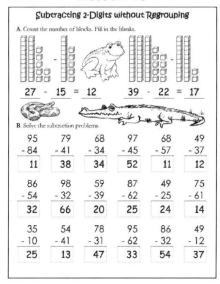

27 - 15 = 12   39 - 22 = 17

B. Solve the subtraction problems.

95	79	68	97	68	49
- 84	- 41	- 34	- 45	- 57	- 37
11	38	34	52	11	12

86	98	59	87	49	75
- 54	- 32	- 39	- 62	- 25	- 61
32	66	20	25	24	14

35	54	78	95	86	49
- 10	- 41	- 31	- 62	- 32	- 12
25	13	47	33	54	37

Lesson 14

Subtracting 1-Digit with Regrouping

A. Count the number of blocks. Fill in the blanks.

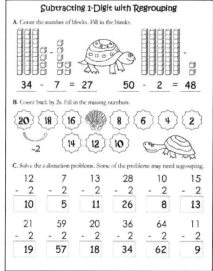

34 - 7 = 27   50 - 2 = 48

B. Count back by 2s. Fill in the missing numbers.

20 18 16 __ 8 6 4 2
-2   14 12 10

C. Solve the subtraction problems. Some of the problems may need regrouping.

12	7	13	28	10	15
- 2	- 2	- 2	- 2	- 2	- 2
10	5	11	26	8	13

21	59	20	36	64	11
- 2	- 2	- 2	- 2	- 2	- 2
19	57	18	34	62	9

Lesson 15

Subtracting 1-Digit with Regrouping

A. Count the number of blocks. Fill in the blanks.

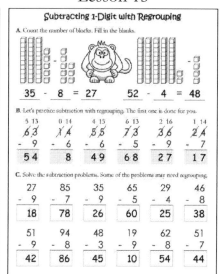

35 - 8 = 27   52 - 4 = 48

B. Let's practice subtraction with regrouping. The first one is done for you.

5 13	0 14	4 15	6 13	2 16	1 14
6̶3̶	1̶4̶	5̶5̶	7̶3̶	3̶6̶	2̶4̶
- 9	- 6	- 6	- 5	- 9	- 7
54	8	49	68	27	17

C. Solve the subtraction problems. Some of the problems may need regrouping.

27	85	35	65	29	46
- 9	- 7	- 9	- 5	- 4	- 8
18	78	26	60	25	38

51	94	48	19	62	51
- 9	- 8	- 3	- 9	- 8	- 7
42	86	45	10	54	44

Lesson 16

Subtracting 2-Digits with Regrouping

A. Count the number of blocks. Fill in the blanks.

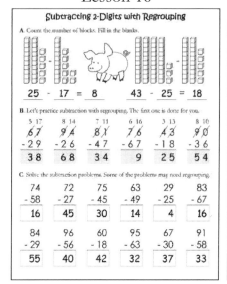

25 - 17 = 8   43 - 25 = 18

B. Let's practice subtraction with regrouping. The first one is done for you.

5 17	8 14	7 11	6 16	3 13	8 10
6̶7̶	9̶4̶	8̶1̶	7̶6̶	4̶3̶	9̶0̶
- 29	- 26	- 47	- 67	- 18	- 36
38	68	34	9	25	54

C. Solve the subtraction problems. Some of the problems may need regrouping.

74	72	75	63	29	83
- 58	- 27	- 45	- 49	- 25	- 67
16	45	30	14	4	16

84	96	60	95	67	91
- 29	- 56	- 18	- 63	- 30	- 58
55	40	42	32	37	33

Lesson 17

Subtraction Word Problems

Solve each word problem. Write the equation and the answer.

Mark had forty-two marbles but lost fifteen of them. How many marbles does Mark have now?
42 - 15 = 27
27 marbles

Bill had 37 marbles. He gave Ethan 13 marbles. How many marbles does Bill have now?
37 - 13 = 24
24 marbles

Owen picked 48 apples, and gave 14 apples to Grace. How many apples does Owen have now?
48 - 14 = 34
34 apples

Emma had fifty-five dimes until she spent thirty-eight of them. How many dimes does Emma have now?
55 - 38 = 17
17 dimes

31 children were wearing hats. 12 children took their hats off. How many children are still wearing their hats?
31 - 12 = 19
19 children

Jenny grew seventy-nine carrots, but the rabbits ate thirty-four carrots. How many carrots does Jenny have left?
79 - 34 = 45
45 carrots

There were thirty-two books on the shelf. Orson took eighteen books from the shelf. How many books are there now?
32 - 18 = 14
14 books

Twenty ducks were swimming in the pond. Thirteen ducks flew away. How many ducks are still swimming in the pond?
20 - 13 = 7
7 ducks

Lesson 18

1-Digit Word Problems

Solve each word problem. Write the equation and the answer.

William ate six grapes. Ethan ate five more grapes than William. How many grapes did Ethan eat?
6 + 5 = 11
11 grapes

Sandy found 7 seashells but 2 were broken. How many unbroken seashells did Sandy find?
7 - 2 = 5
5 seashells

Mark rode his bike 7 miles to the library. Then he rode 6 miles to the park. How many miles did Mark ride altogether?
7 + 6 = 13
13 miles

9 children were wearing hats. 5 children took their hats off. How many children are still wearing their hats?
9 - 5 = 4
4 children

Henry and Samantha ate nine cookies together. Henry ate four cookies. How many cookies did Samantha eat?
9 - 4 = 5
5 cookies

Larry saved $8 last week. He got his allowance on Monday and saved $8 more. How much did Larry save in all?
8 + 8 = 16
16 dollars

Dylan had seven pencils. His brother gave Dylan two more pencils. How many pencils does Dylan have now?
7 + 2 = 9
9 pencils

Jacob and Orson have nine toy cars. Six of the toy cars belong to Jacob. How many toy cars does Orson have?
9 - 6 = 3
3 toy cars

Lesson 19

2-Digit Word Problems

Solve each word problem. Write the equation and the answer.

Tom saw 16 birds on one tree and 12 birds on another tree. How many birds did Tom see in all?

$$16 + 12 = 28$$

28 birds

Jenny had fifty-two dimes. She spent seventeen of her dimes. How many dimes does Jenny have now?

$$52 - 17 = 35$$

35 dimes

Sam has 56 marbles. Leah has 32 marbles. How many more marbles does Sam have than Leah?

$$56 - 32 = 24$$

24 marbles

Henry has fifteen books. Anne has twenty-three books. How many books do they have altogether?

$$15 + 23 = 38$$

38 books

Jacob grew thirty-eight carrots. Orson grew forty-two carrots. How many carrots did they grow in total?

$$38 + 42 = 80$$

80 carrots

Grace has twenty-five stickers. Will has eighteen stickers. How many more stickers does Grace have than Will?

$$25 - 18 = 7$$

7 stickers

Larry read 37 pages of his storybook yesterday. He read 36 pages today. How many pages did Larry read in all?

$$37 + 36 = 73$$

73 pages

Twenty-two children were in the room. Fourteen of them left the room. How many children are still in the room?

$$22 - 14 = 8$$

8 children

Lesson 20

Adding and Subtracting to 20

In each rocket, add or subtract the number in the head to or from each number on the left side. Write the answers on the right side.

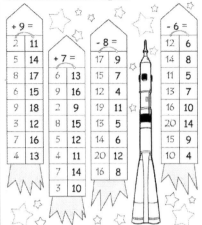

+ 9 =

2	11
5	14
8	17
6	15
9	18
3	12
4	13

+ 7 =

6	13
9	16
2	9
8	15
5	12
4	11
7	14
3	10

- 8 =

17	9
15	7
12	4
19	11
13	5
14	6
20	12
16	8

- 6 =

12	6
14	8
11	5
13	7
16	10
20	14
15	9
10	4

Lesson 21

Counting Coins & Let's Review!

A. Use the fewest number of coins possible to buy each item.

Item	25¢	10¢	5¢	1¢
 8¢	0	0	1	3
17¢	0	1	1	2
49¢	1	2	0	4

B. How much more money would you need to make 100¢?

 + 20 ¢

C. Solve the addition and subtraction problems.

$$420 + 10 = 430 \qquad 160 + 10 = 170$$
$$370 - 10 = 360 \qquad 290 - 10 = 280$$

D. Solve the problems and fill in the blanks.

✓ What is missing? 54, 52, 50, 48, **46, 44, 42**

✓ In 823, what is the value of the 8? **800**

✓ Melanie wants to buy a muffin. It costs 16¢. She has two dimes. Can she buy the muffin? **Yes, she can.**

Lesson 22

Counting Coins & Money Word Problems

A. Color all the pennies brown. Count the coins and write the amount in cents.

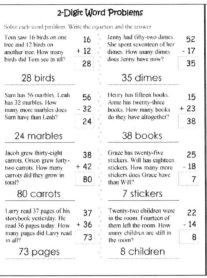

33 ¢   45 ¢   51 ¢

61 ¢   96 ¢   70 ¢

B. Solve each word problem. Write the amount in cents.

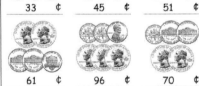

Mark spent 12¢ on a yo-yo and 37¢ on a lollipop. How much did Mark spend in all? **49 ¢**

Alice has 25¢. Kate has 46¢. How much do they have in all? **71 ¢**

Sam has 2 quarters, 2 dimes, 3 nickels, and 2 pennies. How much money does Sam have? **92 ¢**

Lesson 23

Counting Money & Counting by 5s

A. Use the fewest number of bills and coins possible for each amount.

amount	$5	$1	25¢	10¢	5¢	1¢
$1.12	0	1	0	1	0	2
$6.31	1	1	1	0	1	1
$12.69	2	2	2	1	1	4

B. Count by 5s. Fill in the blanks.

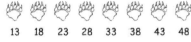

13   18   23   28   33   38   43   48

C. Solve the addition problems.

11	56	5	14	27	5
+ 5	+ 5	+ 25	+ 5	+ 5	+ 63
16	61	30	19	32	68

95	5	42	5	30	109
+ 5	+ 87	+ 5	+ 78	+ 5	+ 5
100	92	47	83	35	114

Lesson 24

Counting Money & Let's Review!

A. Solve each word problem. Write your answer.

The total is $0.92. You have 9 dimes. How many pennies do you need? **2**

The total is $1.55. You have 8 dimes. How many quarters do you need? **3**

The total is $0.95. You have 7 nickels. How many dimes do you need? **6**

B. How much more money would you need to make 100¢?

+ 53 ¢

C. Solve the addition and subtraction problems.

$$623 + 10 = 633 \qquad 478 + 10 = 488$$
$$359 - 10 = 349 \qquad 215 - 10 = 205$$

D. Solve the problems and fill in the blanks.

✓ What comes next? 905, 805, 705, **605, 505, 405**

✓ In 258, what is the value of the 5? **50**

✓ Laura saw 3 cows in the pasture. How many legs did she see? **12**

✓ How many nickels do you need to make 35 cents? **7**

Lesson 25

Counting Money & Subtracting 2-Digits

A. Color all the pennies brown. Write the total amount of money.

 = $35.36

= $20.40

 = $7.16

B. Solve the subtraction problems.

61	74	52	98	70	38
- 32	- 56	- 13	- 34	- 25	- 32
29	18	39	64	45	6

75	83	34	63	92	58
- 37	- 50	- 19	- 25	- 38	- 18
38	33	15	38	54	40

Lesson 26

Money Word Problems

Look at the price of each item and solve the word problems.

Whistle	Candy	Toy Car	Die	Top
$0.24	$0.17	$0.55	$0.16	$0.38

Ava bought one whistle and one toy car. How much money did Ava spend in all? **$0.79**

Grace had $0.55 and spent all of her money on one item. Which item did Grace buy? **toy car**

Kyle bought three candies. How much money did Kyle spend in all? **$0.51**

Orson bought two candies and one top. How much money did Orson spend in total? **$0.72**

Dylan bought one item with two dimes, three nickels, and three pennies. Which item did Dylan buy? **top**

Jacob bought two of the same item with one quarter and seven pennies. Which item did Jacob buy? **die**

If Amber buys three different items, what is the least amount of money Amber can spend? **$0.57**

If Owen buys two different items, what is the most amount of money Owen can spend? **$0.93**

Lesson 27

Making Change & Equal Parts

A. For each item you buy, determine how much change you would receive.

	You buy	You pay	You receive
	$0.10	$1.00	$0.90
	$0.27	$1.00	$0.73
	$0.36	$1.00	$0.64
	$0.55	$1.00	$0.45
	$0.73	$1.00	$0.27
	$0.99	$1.00	$0.01

B. Draw a line to cut each shape into two equal parts.

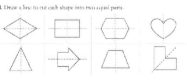

Lesson 28

Making Change

Determine your change for each purchase. Write the equation and the answer.

Peach 20¢ Lemon 35¢ Pear 60¢ Apple 29¢ Banana 10¢

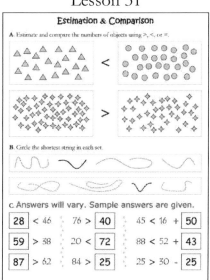

You buy a peach and pay one dollar. What's your change?
100¢ − 20¢ = **80¢**   80¢

You buy a pear with a dollar bill. What's your change?
100¢ − 60¢ = **40¢**   40¢

You buy a banana and pay one dollar. What's your change?
100¢ − 10¢ = **90¢**   90¢

You buy two peaches with a dollar bill. What's your change?
100¢ − 40¢ = **60¢**   60¢

You buy a lemon and pay one dollar. What's your change?
100¢ − 35¢ = **65¢**   65¢

You buy an apple with a dollar bill. What's your change?
100¢ − 29¢ = **71¢**   71¢

You buy two lemons and pay one dollar. What's your change?
100¢ − 70¢ = **30¢**   30¢

You buy two apples with a dollar bill. What's your change?
100¢ − 58¢ = **42¢**   42¢

Lesson 29

Subtracting Money

A. Solve the subtraction problems.

$0.65 − $0.21 = **$0.44**	$0.87 − $0.23 = **$0.64**	$0.47 − $0.12 = **$0.35**	$1.00 − $0.11 = **$0.89**
$0.84 − $0.35 = **$0.49**	$0.35 − $0.27 = **$0.08**	$0.72 − $0.56 = **$0.16**	$0.52 − $0.52 = **$0.00**
$0.95 − $0.78 = **$0.17**	$1.00 − $0.37 = **$0.63**	$0.71 − $0.29 = **$0.42**	$0.85 − $0.38 = **$0.47**

B. Can you solve these money riddles? Choose the correct answer.

a.   b.   c.

I am more than 15 cents. My coins are the same color. What am I? **A**

I am less than a quarter. I make an odd number of cents. What am I? **B**

Lesson 30

Adding 2-Digits with Regrouping

A. Solve the addition problems.

83 + 19 = 102	68 + 62 = 130	65 + 23 = 88	16 + 75 = 91	38 + 58 = 96	39 + 74 = 113
45 + 89 = 134	42 + 67 = 109	28 + 67 = 95	59 + 49 = 108	43 + 26 = 69	81 + 69 = 150
78 + 45 = 123	19 + 68 = 87	15 + 57 = 72	23 + 50 = 73	85 + 35 = 120	46 + 39 = 85

B. Find and circle 6 horizontal hidden addition problems in the grid.

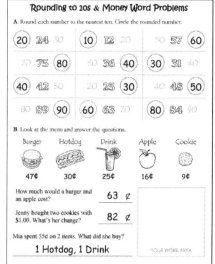

Lesson 31

Estimation & Comparison

A. Estimate and compare the numbers of objects using >, <, or =.

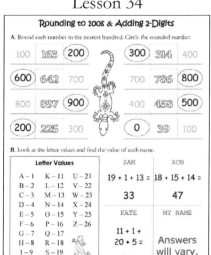

△ **<** ●

◆ **>** ◆

B. Circle the shortest string in each set.

c. Answers will vary. Sample answers are given.

28 **<** 46	76 > **40**	45 < 16 + **50**
59 **>** 38	20 < **72**	88 < 52 + **43**
87 **>** 62	84 > **25**	25 > 30 − **25**

Lesson 32

Rounding to 10s & Money Word Problems

A. Round each number to the nearest ten. Circle the rounded number.

(20) 24 30	(10) 12 20	50 57 (60)
70 75 (80)	50 36 (40)	(30) 31 40
(40) 42 50	20 25 (30)	40 43 (50)
80 89 (90)	(60) 63 70	(80) 84 90

B. Look at the menu and answer the questions.

Burger 47¢   Hotdog 30¢   Drink 25¢   Apple 16¢   Cookie 9¢

How much would a burger and an apple cost? **63** ¢

Jenny bought two cookies with $1.00. What's her change? **82** ¢

Mia spent 55¢ on 2 items. What did she buy? **1 Hotdog, 1 Drink**

YOUR WORK AREA

Lesson 33

Rounding to 10s & Let's Review!

A. Round each number to the nearest ten. Circle the rounded number.

(40) 41 50	70 78 (80)	30 36 (40)
20 25 (30)	10 17 (20)	(80) 82 90
(70) 73 80	(50) 50 60	(60) 64 70

B. Solve the addition and subtraction problems.

145 + 302 = 447	427 + 235 = 662	249 + 100 = 349	756 − 243 = 513	172 − 92 = 80

C. What is the next problem? Find the pattern.

25 + 1	35 + 2	45 + 3	55 + 4	**65 + 5**	**75 + 6**

D. Solve the problems and fill in the blanks.

✓ Measure the length of this workbook from top to bottom. How long is it? **11 inches**

✓ Amber has 16 candies. Her sister has twice as many. How many candies does her sister have? **32 candies**

Lesson 34

Rounding to 100s & Adding 2-Digits

A. Round each number to the nearest hundred. Circle the rounded number.

100 163 (200)	(300) 314 400
(600) 642 700	700 786 (800)
800 897 (900)	400 453 (500)
(200) 225 300	(0) 39 100

B. Look at the letter values and find the value of each name.

Letter Values		
A – 1	K – 11	U – 21
B – 2	L – 12	V – 22
C – 3	M – 13	W – 23
D – 4	N – 14	X – 24
E – 5	O – 15	Y – 25
F – 6	P – 16	Z – 26
G – 7	Q – 17	
H – 8	R – 18	
I – 9	S – 19	
J – 10	T – 20	

SAM: 19 + 1 + 13 = **33**

RON: 18 + 15 + 14 = **47**

KATE: 11 + 1 + 20 + 5 = **37**

MY NAME: Answers will vary.

Lesson 35

Rounding to 10s and 100s

A. Draw lines to match each number to the nearest ten.

54, 73, 32, 78, 39, 94, 56 → 30, 40, 50, 60, 70, 80, 90 → 41, 83, 63, 89, 27, 72, 48

B. Round each number to the nearest hundred. Circle the rounded number.

(300) 329 400	200 275 (300)
500 563 (600)	(0) 26 100
(800) 844 900	(400) 410 500
100 157 (200)	700 782 (800)

Lesson 36

Telling Time: To the Half Hour

What time is it? Write the time underneath each clock.

10:00	2:30	6:00	4:30
5:00	7:30	11:30	2:00
12:30	9:00	5:30	1:00

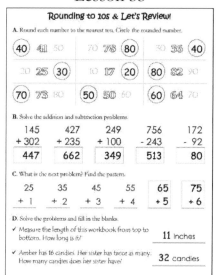

Lesson 37

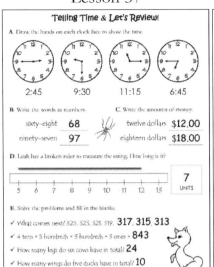

Telling Time & Let's Review!

A. Draw the hands on each clock face to show the time

2:45   9:30   11:15   6:45

B. Write the words as numbers.   C. Write the amounts of money.

sixty-eight **68**   twelve dollars **$12.00**

ninety-seven **97**   eighteen dollars **$18.00**

D. Leah has a broken ruler to measure the string. How long is it?

7 UNITS

5 6 7 8 9 10 11 12 13

E. Solve the problems and fill in the blanks.

✓ What comes next? 325, 323, 321, 319, **317, 315, 313**

✓ 4 tens + 5 hundreds + 3 hundreds + 3 ones = **843**

✓ How many legs do six cows have in total? **24**

✓ How many wings do five ducks have in total? **10**

Lesson 38

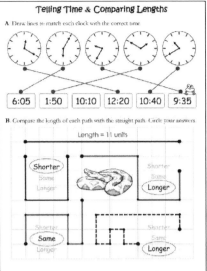

Telling Time & Comparing Lengths

A. Draw lines to match each clock with the correct time.

6:05   1:50   10:10   12:20   10:40   9:35

B. Compare the length of each path with the straight path. Circle your answers.

Length = 11 units

Shorter / Same / **Longer**   Shorter / Same / **Longer**

Same / Longer   Shorter / Same / **Longer**

Lesson 39

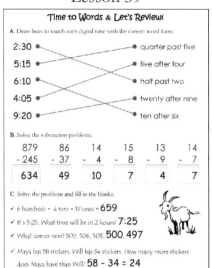

Time to Words & Let's Review!

A. Draw lines to match each digital time with the correct word form.

2:30 •   • quarter past five

5:15 •   • five after four

6:10 •   • half past two

4:05 •   • twenty after nine

9:20 •   • ten after six

B. Solve the subtraction problems.

879	86	14	15	13	14
- 245	- 37	- 4	- 8	- 9	- 7
634	49	10	7	4	7

C. Solve the problems and fill in the blanks.

✓ 6 hundreds + 4 tens + 19 ones = **659**

✓ It's 5:25. What time will be in 2 hours? **7:25**

✓ What comes next? 509, 506, 505, **500, 497**

✓ Maya has 58 stickers. Will has 34 stickers. How many more stickers does Maya have than Will? **58 - 34 = 24**

Lesson 41

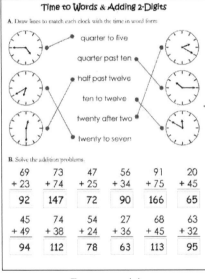

Time to Words & Adding 2-Digits

A. Draw lines to match each clock with the time in word form.

quarter to five
quarter past ten
half past twelve
ten to twelve
twenty after two
twenty to seven

B. Solve the addition problems.

69	73	47	56	91	20
+ 23	+ 74	+ 25	+ 34	+ 75	+ 45
92	147	72	90	166	65

45	74	54	27	68	63
+ 49	+ 38	+ 24	+ 36	+ 45	+ 32
94	112	78	63	113	95

Lesson 42

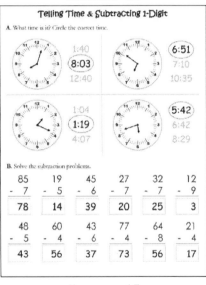

Telling Time & Subtracting 1-Digit

A. What time is it? Circle the correct time.

1:40 / **8:03** / 12:40   **6:51** / 7:10 / 10:35

1:04 / **1:19** / 4:07   **5:42** / 6:42 / 8:29

B. Solve the subtraction problems.

85	19	45	27	32	12
- 7	- 5	- 6	- 7	- 7	- 9
78	14	39	20	25	3

48	60	43	77	64	21
- 5	- 4	- 6	- 4	- 8	- 4
43	56	37	73	56	17

Lesson 43

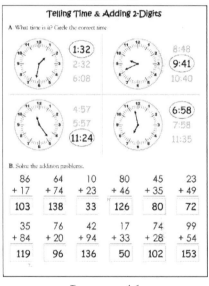

Telling Time & Adding 2-Digits

A. What time is it? Circle the correct time.

1:32 / 2:32 / 6:08   8:48 / **9:41** / 10:40

4:57 / 5:57 / **11:24**   **6:58** / 7:58 / 11:35

B. Solve the addition problems.

86	64	10	80	45	23
+ 17	+ 74	+ 23	+ 46	+ 35	+ 49
103	138	33	126	80	72

35	76	42	17	74	99
+ 84	+ 20	+ 94	+ 33	+ 28	+ 54
119	96	136	50	102	153

Lesson 44

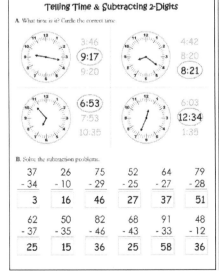

Telling Time & Subtracting 2-Digits

A. What time is it? Circle the correct time.

3:46 / **9:17** / 9:20   4:42 / 8:20 / **8:21**

6:53 / 7:53 / 10:35   6:03 / **12:34** / 1:35

B. Solve the subtraction problems.

37	26	75	52	64	79
- 34	- 10	- 29	- 25	- 27	- 28
3	16	46	27	37	51

62	50	82	68	91	48
- 37	- 35	- 46	- 43	- 33	- 12
25	15	36	25	58	36

Lesson 45

Words to Time & Venn Diagrams

A. Write each time in digital form.

quarter of eight **7:45**   twenty to four **3:40**

five past five **5:05**   eleven past two **2:11**

quarter past six **6:15**   thirteen to twelve **11:47**

quarter to three **2:45**   quarter to eleven **10:45**

half past eleven **11:30**   eighteen past ten **10:18**

B. Use the diagram to answer YES or NO to the questions.

Less than 10   Even
• A   • B   • C
• D

✓ Could A be 15? **NO**
✓ Could B be 8? **YES**
✓ Could C be 10? **YES**
✓ Could D be 9? **NO**

C. Put each number into the appropriate space of the Venn diagram.

102 341
789 926
218 453

Less than 400 / Odd
102 **341** 453
218 **789**
926

Lesson 46

Numbers to 1000 & Adding to 20

A. Match each number word to the number.

Nine hundred fifty-three •   • 839
Eight hundred thirty-nine •   • 782
Seven hundred eighty-two •   • 953

B. Compare the numbers using <, >, or =.

295 < 435	130 < 342	755 = 755
338 > 246	421 = 421	558 > 520
742 > 732	655 > 243	472 < 803

C. Solve the addition problems.

4	+	5	=	9		3	+	4	=	7
+		+		+		+		+		+
2	+	5	=	7		6	+	2	=	8
=		=		=		=		=		=
6	+	10	=	16		9	+	6	=	15

Lesson 47

Place Value & Subtracting to 20

A. Write the numbers in expanded form.

3248 = 3000 + 200 + 40 + 8

2693 = 2000 + 600 + 90 + 3

5827 = 5000 + 800 + 20 + 7

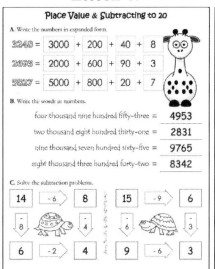

B. Write the words as numbers.

four thousand nine hundred fifty-three = 4953

two thousand eight hundred thirty-one = 2831

nine thousand seven hundred sixty-five = 9765

eight thousand three hundred forty-two = 8342

C. Solve the subtraction problems.

14 − 6 → 8   15 − 9 → 6

− 8 → 6   − 4 → 4   − 6 → 6   − 3 → 3

6 − 2 → 4   9 − 6 → 3

Lesson 48

Place Value & Adding to 20

A. Make numbers using the given place values.

7 Ten thousands 1 Thousand 4 Hundreds 0 Tens 5 Ones	5 Ten thousands 2 Thousands 0 Hundreds 8 Tens 4 Ones	6 Ten thousands 3 Thousands 4 Hundreds 9 Tens 0 Ones
71405	52084	63490
3 Tens 4 Ten thousands 8 Thousands 2 Hundreds 6 Ones	0 Ones 2 Thousands 1 Ten thousand 8 Hundreds 4 Tens	5 Hundreds 6 Ten thousands 3 Thousands 0 Tens 0 Ones
48236	12840	63500

B. Change the order of the digits to make the biggest number possible.

3 1 6 4 5 ⇨ 65431

0 2 5 9 0 ⇨ 95200

C. Complete the addition problems.

7 +4 = 11	7 +8 = 15	8 +9 = 17	6 +6 = 12	5 +8 = 13	4 +9 = 13	3 +8 = 11	9 +6 = 15

Lesson 49

Adding 3-Digits

A. Add 3-digit numbers. Use the base ten blocks from the previous worksheets.

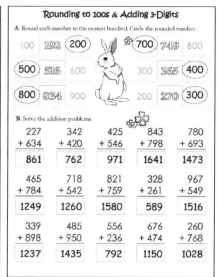

```
  250      1 1
+ 345    3 6 1     1 6 8
 595   + 2 9 7   + 4 5 5
        6 5 8     6 2 3
```

```
  1 1
  7 8 6    7 2 5
+ 3 2 9  + 8 1 2
1 1 1 5  1 5 3 7
```

B. Can you solve these number riddles?

I am an even number. I am between 541 and 550. My ones digit is bigger than my tens digit. The sum of my digits is 15. What number am I?

546

I am a 3-digit number. My ones digit is half of 8. My tens digit is half of my ones digit. The sum of my digits is 13. What number am I?

724

Lesson 50

Adding 3-Digits

Add 3-digit numbers. Use the base ten blocks from **Day 49** to help you.

```
      1
  8 7 5    9 7 6    2 3 5    5 0 6
+ 3 1 4  + 1 2 2  + 6 1 3  + 7 4 8
1 1 8 9  1 0 9 8    8 4 8  1 2 5 4
```

```
    1                1
  6 9 7    2 3 1    4 8 3    4 3 5
+ 5 4 0  + 3 6 8  + 6 7 4  + 1 2 6
1 2 3 7    5 9 9  1 1 5 7    5 6 1
```

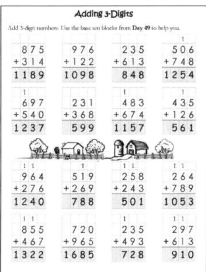

```
  1 1        1     1 1      1 1
  9 6 4    5 1 9    2 5 8    2 6 4
+ 2 7 6  + 2 6 9  + 2 4 3  + 7 8 9
1 2 4 0    7 8 8    5 0 1  1 0 5 3
```

```
  1 1        1              1 1
  8 5 5    7 2 0    2 3 5    2 9 7
+ 4 6 7  + 9 6 5  + 4 9 3  + 6 1 3
1 3 2 2  1 6 8 5    7 2 8    9 1 0
```

Lesson 51

Rounding to 10s & Adding 3-Digits

A. Round each number to the nearest ten. Circle the rounded number.

(50) 52 60   80 57 (90)   40 45 (50)

(10) 13 20   (60) 64 70   20 28 (30)

70 79 (80)   20 26 (30)   (60) 61 70

B. Solve the addition problems.

353 +118 = 471	141 +673 = 814	469 +675 = 1144	234 +153 = 387	573 +485 = 1058
748 +866 = 1614	208 +537 = 745	932 +564 = 1496	873 +865 = 1738	232 +952 = 1184
934 +634 = 1568	461 +343 = 804	889 +578 = 1467	257 +352 = 609	239 +623 = 862

Lesson 52

Rounding to 100s & Adding 3-Digits

A. Round each number to the nearest hundred. Circle the rounded number.

100 192 (200)   (700) 749 800

(500) 516 600   300 365 (400)

(800) 834 900   200 270 (300)

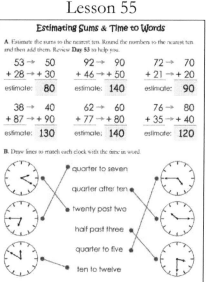

B. Solve the addition problems.

227 +634 = 861	342 +420 = 762	425 +546 = 971	843 +798 = 1641	780 +693 = 1473
465 +784 = 1249	718 +542 = 1260	821 +759 = 1580	328 +261 = 589	967 +549 = 1516
339 +898 = 1237	485 +950 = 1435	556 +236 = 792	676 +474 = 1150	260 +768 = 1028

Lesson 53

Adding 2-Digits & Estimating Sums

A. Solve the addition problems to find the actual sums.

78 +93 = 171	23 +16 = 39	47 +26 = 73	68 +76 = 144	84 +42 = 126	48 +16 = 64

B. Estimate the sums to the nearest ten. Round the numbers to the nearest ten and then add them. The first one is done for you!

78 → 80 / +93 → +90 / estimate: 170

23 → 20 / +16 → +20 / estimate: 40

47 → 50 / +26 → +30 / estimate: 80

68 → 70 / +76 → +80 / estimate: 150

84 → 80 / +42 → +40 / estimate: 120

48 → 50 / +16 → +20 / estimate: 70

C. Compare the actual sums and the estimated sums. Are they good estimates?

Lesson 54

Subtracting 2-Digits & Estimating Differences

A. Solve the subtraction problems to find the actual differences.

76 −21 = 55	64 −47 = 17	88 −16 = 72	70 −27 = 43	52 −28 = 24	71 −56 = 15

B. Estimate the differences to the nearest ten. Round the numbers to the nearest ten and then subtract them. The first one is done for you!

76 → 80 / −21 → −20 / estimate: 60

64 → 60 / −47 → −50 / estimate: 10

88 → 90 / −16 → −20 / estimate: 70

70 → 70 / −27 → −30 / estimate: 40

52 → 50 / −28 → −30 / estimate: 20

71 → 70 / −56 → −60 / estimate: 10

C. Compare the actual differences and the estimated differences. Are they good estimates?

Lesson 55

Estimating Sums & Time to Words

A. Estimate the sums to the nearest ten. Round the numbers to the nearest ten and then add them. Review **Day 53** to help you.

53 → 50 / +28 → +30 / estimate: 80

92 → 90 / +46 → +50 / estimate: 140

72 → 70 / +21 → +20 / estimate: 90

38 → 40 / +87 → +90 / estimate: 130

62 → 60 / +77 → +80 / estimate: 140

76 → 80 / +35 → +40 / estimate: 120

B. Draw lines to match each clock with the time in word.

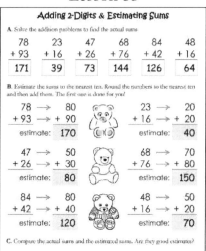

quarter to seven

quarter after ten

twenty post two

half past three

quarter to five

ten to twelve

Lesson 56

Estimating Sums & Subtracting to 20

A. Estimate the sums by rounding the numbers to the nearest ten. Solve the actual problems as well. Review **Day 53** to help you.

36 → 40	93 → 90	55 → 60
+ 45 → + 50	+ 18 → + 20	+ 75 → + 80
81 90	**111 110**	**130 140**

61 → 60	80 → 80	42 → 40
+ 87 → + 90	+ 54 → + 50	+ 34 → + 30
148 150	**134 130**	**76 70**

22 → 20	76 → 80	47 → 50
+ 61 → + 60	+ 27 → + 30	+ 34 → + 30
83 80	**103 110**	**81 80**

B. Solve the subtraction problems.

19 −5 14 −3 11 −2 9
−3 −2 −3 −4
16 −4 12 −4 8 −3 5

Lesson 57

Estimating Differences & Counting Coins

A. Estimate the differences by rounding the numbers to the nearest ten. Solve the actual problems as well. Review **Day 54** to help you.

58 → 60	72 → 70	56 → 60
− 32 → − 30	− 50 → − 50	− 25 → − 30
26 30	**22 20**	**31 30**

79 → 80	89 → 90	78 → 80
− 64 → − 60	− 42 → − 40	− 36 → − 40
15 20	**47 50**	**42 40**

95 → 100	67 → 70	97 → 100
− 23 → − 20	− 56 → − 60	− 34 → − 30
72 80	**11 10**	**63 70**

B. Write the total amounts in cents.

2 dimes + 5 nickels + 2 pennies = **47 ¢**
1 quarter + 3 dimes + 4 pennies = **59 ¢**
2 quarters + 3 nickels + 8 pennies = **73 ¢**
1 quarter + 4 dimes + 5 nickels + 5 pennies = **95 ¢**

Lesson 58

Estimating Sums & Telling Time

A. Estimate the sums by rounding the numbers to the nearest ten. Solve the actual problems as well. Review **Day 53** to help you.

42 → 40	53 → 50	89 → 90
+ 38 → + 40	+ 82 → + 80	+ 75 → + 80
80 80	**135 130**	**164 170**

23 → 20	67 → 70	85 → 90
+ 43 → + 40	+ 54 → + 50	+ 67 → + 70
66 60	**121 120**	**152 160**

50 → 50	76 → 80	91 → 90
+ 35 → + 40	+ 23 → + 20	+ 62 → + 60
85 90	**99 100**	**153 150**

B. What time is it? Write the time underneath each clock.

6:55   **12:34**   **8:21**

Lesson 59

Estimating Differences & Comparing Numbers

A. Estimate the differences by rounding the numbers to the nearest ten. Solve the actual problems as well. Review **Day 54** to help you.

59 → 60	83 → 80	92 → 90
− 27 → − 30	− 50 → − 50	− 45 → − 50
32 30	**33 30**	**47 40**

60 → 60	83 → 80	58 → 60
− 54 → − 50	− 17 → − 20	− 15 → − 20
6 10	**66 60**	**43 40**

67 → 70	54 → 50	92 → 90
− 23 → − 20	− 36 → − 40	− 68 → − 70
44 50	**18 10**	**24 20**

B. For each pair, circle the greater number.

122 (344)	670 (760)	786 (876)
(535) 232	278 (540)	345 (456)
400 (500)	(455) 445	(605) 506
755 (758)	234 (392)	(770) 570

Lesson 60

3-D Shapes & Place Value

A. Draw lines to match the shapes and their names.

Sphere   Cone   Pyramid   Cube   Cylinder   Cuboid

B. Write the number of blocks in each set.

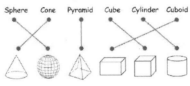

2150

1237

3045

Lesson 61

Subtracting 3-Digits

A. Subtract 3-digit numbers. Use the base ten blocks from **Day 49** to help you.

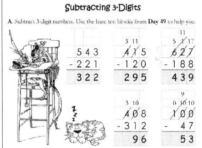

543	415	627
− 221	− 120	− 188
322	**295**	**439**

408	100	
− 312	− 47	
96	**53**	

B. Can you solve these number riddles?

I am an odd number. I am between 365 and 375. My tens digit is bigger than my ones digit. The sum of my digits is 13. What number am I?

373

I am a 3-digit number. My ones digit is half of 16. My tens digit is half of my ones digit. The sum of my digits is 18. What number am I?

648

Lesson 62

Subtracting 3-Digits

Subtract 3-digit numbers. Use the base ten blocks from **Day 49** to help you.

862	773	842	951
− 474	− 556	− 468	− 323
388	**217**	**374**	**628**

769	843	984	562
− 334	− 697	− 128	− 235
435	**146**	**856**	**327**

650	532	478	736
− 536	− 259	− 224	− 695
114	**273**	**254**	**41**

Lesson 63

Subtracting 3-Digits

Subtract 3-digit numbers. Use the base ten blocks from **Day 49** to help you.

357	472	748	821
− 126	− 328	− 374	− 564
231	**144**	**374**	**257**

232	799	773	712
− 156	− 145	− 459	− 639
76	**654**	**314**	**73**

589	657	325	943
− 247	− 485	− 243	− 268
342	**172**	**82**	**675**

Lesson 64

Subtracting 3-Digits

Subtract 3-digit numbers. Use the base ten blocks from **Day 49** to help you.

923	782	952	934
− 832	− 206	− 287	− 562
91	**576**	**665**	**372**

461	679	731	590
− 359	− 324	− 257	− 453
102	**355**	**474**	**137**

628	745	278	472
− 565	− 389	− 154	− 237
63	**356**	**124**	**235**

Lesson 65

Patterns & Place Value

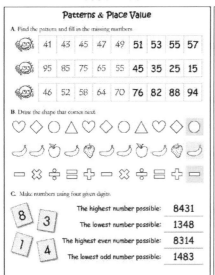

A. Find the pattern and fill in the missing numbers.

| 41 | 43 | 45 | 47 | 49 | 51 | 53 | 55 | 57 |

| 95 | 85 | 75 | 65 | 55 | 45 | 35 | 25 | 15 |

| 46 | 52 | 58 | 64 | 70 | 76 | 82 | 88 | 94 |

B. Draw the shape that comes next.

C. Make numbers using four given digits.

8 3 1 4

The highest number possible:	8431
The lowest number possible:	1348
The highest even number possible:	8314
The lowest odd number possible:	1483

Lesson 66

Rounding/Estimation with Hundreds

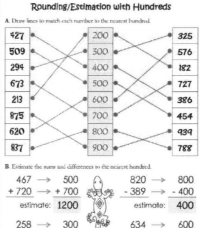

A. Draw lines to match each number to the nearest hundred.

427, 509, 294, 673, 213, 875, 620, 837

200, 300, 400, 500, 600, 700, 800, 900

325, 576, 182, 727, 386, 454, 939, 788

B. Estimate the sums and differences to the nearest hundred.

467 → 500	820 → 800
+ 720 → + 700	- 389 → - 400
estimate: 1200	estimate: 400

258 → 300	634 → 600
+ 802 → + 800	- 379 → - 400
estimate: 1100	estimate: 200

Lesson 67

Estimating Sums & Adding 3-Digits

Estimate the sums by rounding the numbers to the nearest hundred. Solve the actual problems as well.

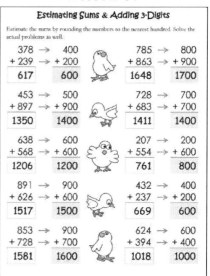

378 → 400	785 → 800
+ 239 → + 200	+ 863 → + 900
617	600	1648	1700

453 → 500	728 → 700
+ 897 → + 900	+ 683 → + 700
1350	1400	1411	1400

638 → 600	207 → 200
+ 568 → + 600	+ 554 → + 600
1206	1200	761	800

891 → 900	432 → 400
+ 626 → + 600	+ 237 → + 200
1517	1500	669	600

853 → 900	624 → 600
+ 728 → + 700	+ 394 → + 400
1581	1600	1018	1000

Lesson 68

Estimating Differences & Subtracting 3-Digits

Estimate the differences by rounding the numbers to the nearest hundred. Solve the actual problems as well.

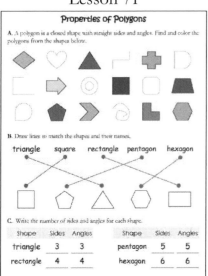

928 → 900	647 → 600
- 524 → - 500	- 290 → - 300
404	400	357	300

896 → 900	827 → 800
- 134 → - 100	- 562 → - 600
762	800	265	200

761 → 800	743 → 700
- 438 → - 400	- 286 → - 300
323	400	457	400

441 → 400	835 → 800
- 373 → - 400	- 329 → - 300
68	0	506	500

750 → 800	881 → 900
- 195 → - 200	- 207 → - 200
555	600	674	700

Lesson 69

Estimating Sums & Adding 3-Digits

Estimate the sums by rounding the numbers to the nearest hundred. Solve the actual problems as well.

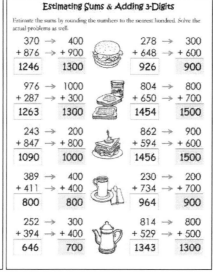

370 → 400	278 → 300
+ 876 → + 900	+ 648 → + 600
1246	1300	926	900

976 → 1000	804 → 800
+ 287 → + 300	+ 650 → + 700
1263	1300	1454	1500

243 → 200	862 → 900
+ 847 → + 800	+ 594 → + 600
1090	1000	1456	1500

389 → 400	230 → 200
+ 411 → + 400	+ 734 → + 700
800	800	964	900

252 → 300	814 → 800
+ 394 → + 400	+ 529 → + 500
646	700	1343	1300

Lesson 70

Estimating Differences & Subtracting 3-Digits

Estimate the differences by rounding the numbers to the nearest hundred. Solve the actual problems as well.

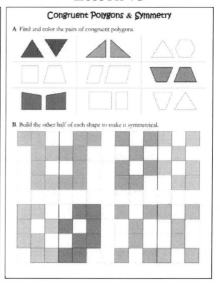

724 → 700	527 → 500
- 342 → - 300	- 105 → - 100
382	400	422	400

632 → 600	612 → 600
- 594 → - 600	- 451 → - 500
38	0	161	100

866 → 900	813 → 800
- 439 → - 400	- 458 → - 500
427	500	355	300

462 → 500	923 → 900
- 386 → - 400	- 285 → - 300
76	100	638	600

626 → 600	942 → 900
- 354 → - 400	- 728 → - 700
272	200	214	200

Lesson 71

Properties of Polygons

A. A polygon is a closed shape with straight sides and angles. Find and color the polygons from the shapes below.

B. Draw lines to match the shapes and their names.

triangle   square   rectangle   pentagon   hexagon

C. Write the number of sides and angles for each shape.

Shape	Sides	Angles
triangle	3	3
rectangle	4	4

Shape	Sides	Angles
pentagon	5	5
hexagon	6	6

Lesson 72

Congruent Shapes & Symmetry

A. Find and color the pairs of congruent shapes.

B. Draw a line of symmetry on each shape

M A K E

C. Draw the other half of each picture to make it symmetrical.

Lesson 73

Congruent Polygons & Symmetry

A. Find and color the pairs of congruent polygons.

B. Build the other half of each shape to make it symmetrical.

Lesson 74

Perimeter of a Shape

A. Calculate the perimeter of each shape.

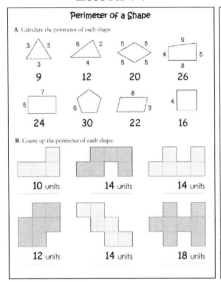

9   12   20   26

24   30   22   16

B. Count up the perimeter of each shape.

10 units   14 units   14 units

12 units   14 units   18 units

Lesson 75

Perimeter & Geometry Terms

A. Count up the perimeter of each shape.

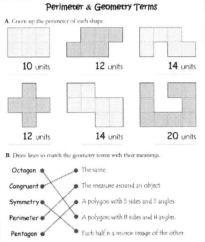

10 units   12 units   14 units

12 units   14 units   20 units

B. Draw lines to match the geometry terms with their meanings.

Octagon ●   ● The same

Congruent ●   ● The measure around an object

Symmetry ●   ● A polygon with 5 sides and 5 angles.

Perimeter ●   ● A polygon with 8 sides and 8 angles.

Pentagon ●   ● Each half is a mirror image of the other.

Polygon ●   ● A closed shape with straight sides and angles.

Lesson 76

Place Value, Rounding & 3D Shapes

A. Write the number in expanded form.

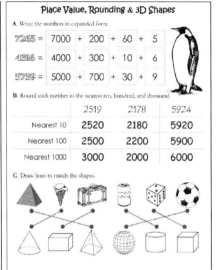

7265 = 7000 + 200 + 60 + 5

4316 = 4000 + 300 + 10 + 6

5739 = 5000 + 700 + 30 + 9

B. Round each number to the nearest ten, hundred, and thousand.

	2519	2178	5924
Nearest 10	2520	2180	5920
Nearest 100	2500	2200	5900
Nearest 1000	3000	2000	6000

C. Draw lines to match the shapes.

Lesson 77

Rounding to 10s and 100s & Subtracting to 20

A. Round each number to the nearest ten.

31	30	758	760	3017	3020
57	60	325	330	6343	6340
64	60	102	100	9832	9830
28	30	456	460	4599	4600

B. Round each number to the nearest hundred.

272	300	359	400	2938	2900
694	700	926	900	1642	1600
413	400	177	200	7163	7200
725	700	840	800	3985	4000

C. Solve the subtraction problems.

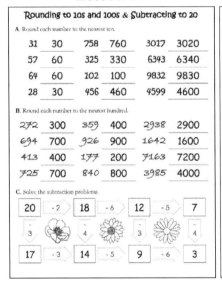

Lesson 78

Estimating Sums & Adding to 20

A. Estimate the sums to the nearest thousand. Round the numbers to the nearest thousand and then add them.

7713 → 8000
+ 5330 → + 5000
estimate: 13000

2032 → 2000
+ 8485 → + 8000
estimate: 10000

4983 → 5000
+ 2487 → + 2000
estimate: 7000

5538 → 6000
+ 4869 → + 5000
estimate: 11000

5252 → 5000
+ 6653 → + 7000
estimate: 12000

9476 → 9000
+ 4348 → + 4000
estimate: 13000

B. Each number is the sum of the two numbers below it. Fill in the hexagons.

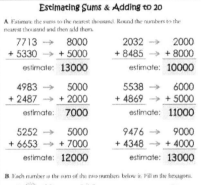

Lesson 79

Estimating Sums & Subtracting to 20

A. Estimate the sums to the nearest thousand. Round the numbers to the nearest thousand and then add them.

5588 → 6000
+ 2857 → + 3000
estimate: 9000

9027 → 9000
+ 8045 → + 8000
estimate: 17000

8756 → 9000
+ 4163 → + 4000
estimate: 13000

2396 → 2000
+ 4364 → + 4000
estimate: 6000

4327 → 4000
+ 6846 → + 7000
estimate: 11000

5242 → 5000
+ 3493 → + 3000
estimate: 8000

B. Connect the problems to their correct answers.

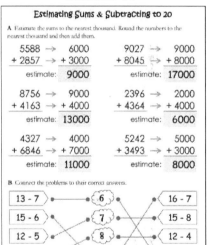

13 - 7 ●   ● 6 ●   ● 16 - 7

15 - 6 ●   ● 7 ●   ● 15 - 8

12 - 5 ●   ● 8 ●   ● 12 - 4

17 - 9 ●   ● 9 ●   ● 14 - 8

Lesson 80

Estimation Practice & Adding to 20

A. Estimate each sum or difference by rounding to the greatest place value.

65 → 70
+ 79 → + 80
estimate: 150

92 → 90
- 58 → - 60
estimate: 30

538 → 500
+ 372 → + 400
estimate: 900

87 → 90
- 29 → - 30
estimate: 60

38 → 40
+ 74 → + 70
estimate: 110

814 → 800
- 658 → - 700
estimate: 100

493 → 500
+ 236 → + 200
estimate: 700

3785 → 4000
+ 3063 → + 3000
estimate: 7000

732 → 700
- 286 → - 300
estimate: 400

5385 → 5000
- 1708 → - 2000
estimate: 3000

B. Solve the addition problems.

7	9	8	4	6	9	8	7
+9	+3	+5	+6	+7	+9	+3	+2
16	12	13	10	13	18	11	9

Lesson 81

Estimating Sums & Adding 4-Digits

A. Estimate the sums by rounding the numbers to the nearest hundred.

8584 → 8600
+ 3205 → + 3200
11789   11800

9228 → 9200
+ 6158 → + 6200
15386   15400

3928 → 3900
+ 6249 → + 6200
10177   10100

7868 → 7900
+ 4762 → + 4800
12630   12700

B. Estimate the sums by rounding the numbers to the nearest thousand.

4352 → 4000
+ 6787 → + 7000
11139   11000

8334 → 8000
+ 5607 → + 6000
13941   14000

2983 → 3000
+ 6065 → + 6000
9048   9000

7554 → 8000
+ 7456 → + 7000
15010   15000

C. Choose four problems above to find the exact sums. You can solve all eight problems if you want!

Lesson 82

Estimating Differences & Subtracting 4-Digits

A. Estimate the differences by rounding the numbers to the nearest hundred.

4665 → 4700
- 1258 → - 1300
3407   3400

8578 → 8600
- 4937 → - 4900
3641   3700

5930 → 5900
- 1675 → - 1700
4255   4200

7278 → 7300
- 3693 → - 3700
3585   3600

B. Estimate the differences by rounding the numbers to the nearest thousand.

8362 → 8000
- 5756 → - 6000
2606   2000

7432 → 7000
- 5867 → - 6000
1565   1000

9116 → 9000
- 6569 → - 7000
2547   2000

5819 → 6000
- 2982 → - 3000
2837   3000

C. Choose four problems above to find the exact differences. You can solve all eight problems if you want!

Lesson 83

Estimating Sums & Adding 4-Digits

A. Estimate the sums by rounding the numbers to the nearest hundred.

$5275 \rightarrow 5300$
$+ 5386 \rightarrow + 5400$
$10661 \quad 10700$

$2875 \rightarrow 2900$
$+ 7260 \rightarrow + 7300$
$10135 \quad 10200$

$5468 \rightarrow 5500$
$+ 7882 \rightarrow + 7900$
$13350 \quad 13400$

$4946 \rightarrow 4900$
$+ 8563 \rightarrow + 8600$
$13509 \quad 13500$

B. Estimate the sums by rounding the numbers to the nearest thousand.

$8250 \rightarrow 8000$
$+ 5279 \rightarrow + 5000$
$13529 \quad 13000$

$9719 \rightarrow 10000$
$+ 3755 \rightarrow + 4000$
$13474 \quad 14000$

$7253 \rightarrow 7000$
$+ 6564 \rightarrow + 7000$
$13817 \quad 14000$

$6189 \rightarrow 6000$
$+ 5067 \rightarrow + 5000$
$11256 \quad 11000$

C. Choose four problems above to find the exact sums. You can solve all eight problems if you want!

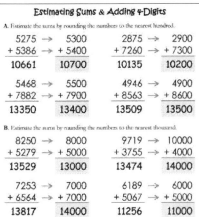

Lesson 84

Estimating Differences & Subtracting 4-Digits

A. Estimate the differences by rounding the numbers to the nearest hundred.

$8752 \rightarrow 8800$
$- 5434 \rightarrow - 5400$
$3318 \quad 3400$

$9459 \rightarrow 9500$
$- 2825 \rightarrow - 2800$
$6634 \quad 6700$

$7422 \rightarrow 7400$
$- 4585 \rightarrow - 4600$
$2837 \quad 2800$

$8050 \rightarrow 8100$
$- 2537 \rightarrow - 2500$
$5513 \quad 5600$

B. Estimate the differences by rounding the numbers to the nearest thousand.

$6720 \rightarrow 7000$
$- 3594 \rightarrow - 4000$
$3126 \quad 3000$

$9126 \rightarrow 9000$
$- 3471 \rightarrow - 3000$
$5655 \quad 6000$

$8723 \rightarrow 9000$
$- 5369 \rightarrow - 5000$
$3354 \quad 4000$

$2244 \rightarrow 2000$
$- 1570 \rightarrow - 2000$
$674 \quad 0$

C. Choose four problems above to find the exact differences. You can solve all eight problems if you want!

Lesson 85

Addition Squares

Add the numbers from left to right and top to bottom to fill in the blanks.

7	4	11
6	8	14
13	12	25

5	8	13
9	8	17
14	16	30

12	23	35
34	35	69
46	58	104

47	22	69
29	58	87
76	80	156

270	314	584
637	103	740
907	417	1324

401	436	837
126	531	657
527	967	1494

371	414	785
326	558	884
697	972	1669

Lesson 86

Elapsed Time & Adding 2-Digits

A. Draw the clock hands to show the passage of time.

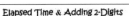
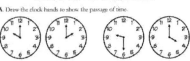

What time will it be in 4 hours?

What time will it be in 6 hours 30 minutes?

What time will it be in 3 hours 15 minutes?

What time will it be in 7 hours 40 minutes?

B. Follow the chain of addition problems. Fill in the ovals.

10 → +5 → 15 → +6 → 21 → +8 → 29
↓ +18   ↓ +27   ↓ +29   ↓ +35
28   42   50   64

Lesson 87

Elapsed Time & Subtracting 2-Digits

A. Draw the clock hands to show the passage of time.

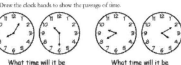

What time will it be in 2 hours 25 minutes?

What time will it be in 6 hours 30 minutes?

What time will it be in 10 hours 15 minutes?

What time will it be in 11 hours 55 minutes?

B. Follow the chain of subtraction problems. Fill in the ovals.

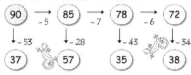

90 → −5 → 85 → −7 → 78 → −6 → 72
↓ −53   ↓ −28   ↓ −43   ↓ −34
37   57   35   38

Lesson 88

Elapsed Time & Adding to 20

A. Write the time for each clock and calculate the elapsed time.

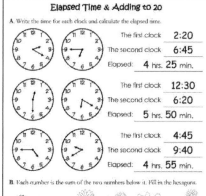

The first clock **2:20**
The second clock **6:45**
Elapsed: **4** hrs. **25** min.

The first clock **12:30**
The second clock **6:20**
Elapsed: **5** hrs. **50** min.

The first clock **4:45**
The second clock **9:40**
Elapsed: **4** hrs. **55** min.

B. Each number is the sum of the two numbers below it. Fill in the hexagons.

16 / 9 7 / 4 5 2

15 / 7 8 / 3 4 4

14 / 5 9 / 2 3 6

Lesson 89

Elapsed Time & Subtracting to 20

A. Write the time for each clock and calculate the elapsed time.

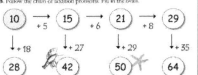

The first clock **11:10**
The second clock **7:30**
Elapsed: **8** hrs. **20** min.

The first clock **12:50**
The second clock **6:40**
Elapsed: **5** hrs. **50** min.

The first clock **7:45**
The second clock **5:20**
Elapsed: **9** hrs. **35** min.

B. Solve the subtraction problems.

20 → −4 → 16 → −4 → 12 → −4 → 8
↓ 2   ↓ 3   ↓ 5   ↓ 4
18 → −5 → 13 → −6 → 7 → −3 → 4

Lesson 90

Reading Charts & Word Problems

A. Read the chart to fill in the blanks.

TIME	ACTIVITY
9:00 – 9:45	Math
9:45 – 10:00	Break
10:00 – 11:00	Reading
11:00 – 11:30	Break
11:30 – 12:20	Computer
12:20 – 1:30	Lunch

Math class starts at **9:00**.
Math class lasts **45** minutes.
Reading class lasts **60** minutes.
The second break ends at **11:30**.
The total break time is **45** minutes.
Lunch starts **50** minutes after Computer class began.

B. Solve each word problem. Write your answer.

Naomi solved 26 problems during the math class. Larry solved 28 problems. How many problems did they solve altogether?

54 problems

Bill has forty-seven blue marbles. Ethan has sixteen more blue marbles than Bill. How many blue marbles does Ethan have?

63 marbles

Derek had seventy-three smiley stickers. He gave twenty-seven of them to his younger sister. How many stickers does Derek have now?

46 stickers

Angela read thirty-five pages of her storybook. Abigail read eighteen pages of her storybook. How many fewer pages did Abigail read?

17 pages

Lesson 91

Fractions of a Whole & Adding 2-Digits

A. Color in the pizza slices to show the fraction.

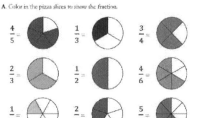

$\frac{4}{5}$ $\frac{1}{3}$ $\frac{3}{4}$

$\frac{2}{3}$ $\frac{1}{2}$ $\frac{4}{6}$

$\frac{1}{6}$ $\frac{2}{5}$ $\frac{5}{8}$

B. Solve the addition puzzle. Use the space on the right for your work area.

16	+	24	=	40
+		+		+
17	+	38	=	55
=		=		=
33	+	62	=	95

Lesson 92

Equivalent Fractions & Subtracting 2-Digits

A. Color in the shapes to find the missing numbers in the equivalent fractions.

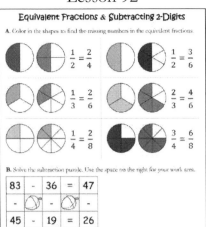

$\frac{1}{2} = \frac{2}{4}$ $\frac{1}{2} = \frac{3}{6}$

$\frac{1}{3} = \frac{2}{6}$ $\frac{2}{3} = \frac{4}{6}$

$\frac{1}{4} = \frac{2}{8}$ $\frac{3}{4} = \frac{6}{8}$

B. Solve the subtraction puzzle. Use the space on the right for your work area.

83	-	36	=	47
-		-		-
45	-	19	=	26
=		=		=
38	-	17	=	21

Lesson 93

Fractions of a Group & Adding 2-Digits

A. Write the fraction that represents the shaded parts of each group.

$\frac{2}{3}$ $\frac{1}{4}$

$\frac{2}{4}$ $\frac{2}{5}$

$\frac{3}{4}$ $\frac{3}{5}$

$\frac{1}{3}$ $\frac{4}{7}$

B. Solve the addition puzzle. Use the space on the right for your work area.

27	+	28	=	55
+		+		+
16	+	19	=	35
=		=		=
43	+	47	=	90

Lesson 94

Equivalent Fractions & Subtracting 2-Digits

A. Color in the shapes to find the missing numbers in the equivalent fractions.

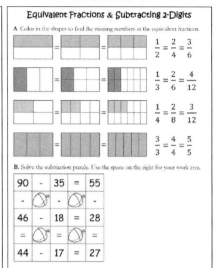

$\frac{1}{2} = \frac{2}{4} = \frac{3}{6}$

$\frac{1}{3} = \frac{2}{6} = \frac{4}{12}$

$\frac{1}{4} = \frac{2}{8} = \frac{3}{12}$

$\frac{3}{3} = \frac{4}{4} = \frac{5}{5}$

B. Solve the subtraction puzzle. Use the space on the right for your work area.

90	-	35	=	55
-		-		-
46	-	18	=	28
=		=		=
44	-	17	=	27

Lesson 95

Geometry Terms & Elapsed Time

A. Draw lines to match the geometry terms with their meanings.

Octagon — The same

Congruent — The measure around an object

Symmetry — A polygon with 5 sides and 5 angles.

Perimeter — A polygon with 8 sides and 8 angles.

Pentagon — Each half is a mirror image of the other.

Polygon — A closed shape with straight sides and angles.

B. Find the elapsed time to complete the table.

Start Time	End Time	Elapsed Time
5:00	10:30	7 hours 30 minutes
4:30	11:15	6 hours 45 minutes
2:15	6:45	4 hours 30 minutes
11:45	3:00	3 hours 15 minutes
9:30	5:45	8 hours 15 minutes
1:45	12:15	10 hours 30 minutes

Lesson 96

Fractions of a Whole & Adding 3-Digits

A. Color in the shape to show the fraction.

$\frac{1}{2}$ $\frac{3}{5}$ $\frac{2}{4}$

$\frac{2}{3}$ $\frac{7}{10}$ $\frac{1}{3}$

$\frac{4}{8}$ $\frac{1}{2}$ $\frac{5}{9}$

B. Solve the addition problems.

547	240	573	452	815
+ 295	+ 586	+ 459	+ 326	+ 635
842	826	1032	778	1450

584	832	168
+ 657	+ 876	+ 532
1241	1708	700

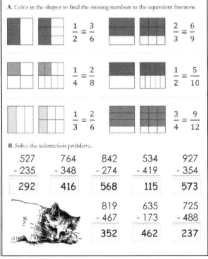

Lesson 97

Equivalent Fractions & Subtracting 3-Digits

A. Color in the shapes to find the missing numbers in the equivalent fractions.

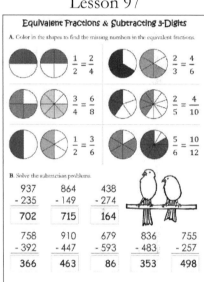

$\frac{1}{2} = \frac{2}{4}$ $\frac{2}{3} = \frac{4}{6}$

$\frac{3}{4} = \frac{6}{8}$ $\frac{2}{5} = \frac{4}{10}$

$\frac{1}{2} = \frac{3}{6}$ $\frac{5}{6} = \frac{10}{12}$

B. Solve the subtraction problems.

937	864	438
- 235	- 149	- 274
702	715	164

758	910	679	836	755
- 392	- 447	- 593	- 483	- 257
366	463	86	353	498

Lesson 98

Equivalent Fractions & Adding 3-Digits

A. Color in the shapes to find the missing numbers in the equivalent fractions.

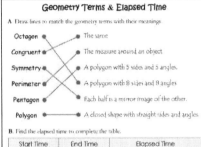

$\frac{1}{2} = \frac{2}{4}$ $\frac{3}{5} = \frac{6}{10}$

$\frac{1}{4} = \frac{2}{8}$ $\frac{1}{3} = \frac{2}{6}$

$\frac{2}{3} = \frac{6}{9}$ $\frac{3}{6} = \frac{6}{12}$

B. Solve the addition problems.

546	247	537
+ 385	+ 540	+ 559
931	787	1096

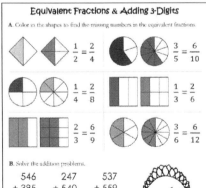

487	524	250	764	746
+ 354	+ 476	+ 594	+ 942	+ 557
841	1000	844	1706	1303

Lesson 99

Equivalent Fractions & Subtracting 3-Digits

A. Color in the shapes to find the missing numbers in the equivalent fractions.

$\frac{1}{2} = \frac{3}{6}$ $\frac{2}{3} = \frac{6}{9}$

$\frac{1}{4} = \frac{2}{8}$ $\frac{1}{2} = \frac{5}{10}$

$\frac{1}{3} = \frac{2}{6}$ $\frac{3}{4} = \frac{9}{12}$

B. Solve the subtraction problems.

527	764	842	534	927
- 235	- 348	- 274	- 419	- 354
292	416	568	115	573

819	635	725
- 467	- 173	- 488
352	462	237

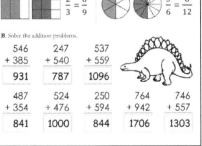

Lesson 100

Math Terms & Symmetric Patterns

A. Draw lines to match the math terms and their meanings.

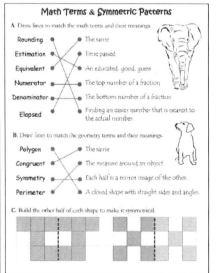

Rounding — The same

Estimation — Time passed

Equivalent — An educated, good, guess

Numerator — The top number of a fraction

Denominator — The bottom number of a fraction

Elapsed — Finding an easier number that is nearest to the actual number.

B. Draw lines to match the geometry terms and their meanings.

Polygon — The same

Congruent — The measure around an object

Symmetry — Each half is a mirror image of the other.

Perimeter — A closed shape with straight sides and angles.

C. Build the other half of each shape to make it symmetrical.

Lesson 101

Comparing Fractions & Adding 2-Digits

A. Color in the shapes to compare the fractions using >, <, or =.

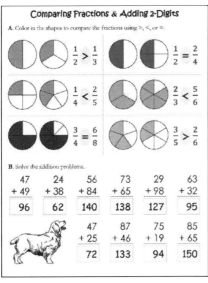

$\frac{1}{2} > \frac{1}{3}$ $\frac{1}{2} = \frac{2}{4}$

$\frac{1}{4} < \frac{2}{5}$ $\frac{2}{3} < \frac{5}{6}$

$\frac{3}{4} = \frac{6}{8}$ $\frac{3}{5} > \frac{2}{6}$

B. Solve the addition problems.

47	24	56	73	29	63
+ 49	+ 38	+ 84	+ 65	+ 98	+ 32
96	62	140	138	127	95

	47	87	75	85
	+ 25	+ 46	+ 19	+ 65
	72	133	94	150

Lesson 102

Comparing Fractions & Subtracting 2-Digits

A. Color in the shapes to compare the fractions using >, <, or =.

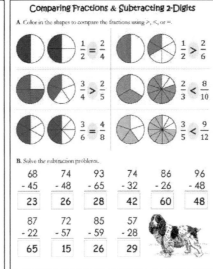

$\frac{1}{2} = \frac{2}{4}$ $\frac{1}{2} > \frac{2}{6}$

$\frac{3}{4} > \frac{2}{5}$ $\frac{2}{3} < \frac{8}{10}$

$\frac{3}{6} = \frac{4}{8}$ $\frac{3}{5} < \frac{9}{12}$

B. Solve the subtraction problems.

68	74	93	74	86	96
- 45	- 48	- 65	- 32	- 26	- 48
23	26	28	42	60	48

87	72	85	57
- 22	- 57	- 59	- 28
65	15	26	29

Lesson 103

Comparing Fractions & Rounding Numbers

A. Color in the shapes to compare the fractions using >, <, or =.

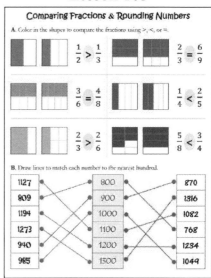

$\frac{1}{2} > \frac{1}{3}$ $\frac{2}{3} = \frac{6}{9}$

$\frac{3}{6} = \frac{4}{8}$ $\frac{1}{4} < \frac{2}{5}$

$\frac{2}{3} > \frac{2}{6}$ $\frac{5}{8} < \frac{3}{4}$

B. Draw lines to match each number to the nearest hundred.

1127		800		870
809		900		1316
1194		1000		1082
1273		1100		768
940		1200		1234
985		1300		1049

Lesson 104

Comparing Fractions & Rounding Numbers

A. Compare the fractions. Use the circles to draw and see the fractions!

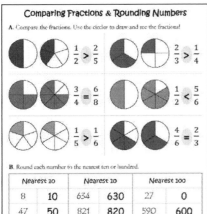

$\frac{1}{2} > \frac{2}{5}$ $\frac{2}{3} > \frac{1}{4}$

$\frac{3}{4} = \frac{6}{8}$ $\frac{1}{2} < \frac{5}{6}$

$\frac{1}{5} > \frac{1}{6}$ $\frac{4}{6} = \frac{2}{3}$

B. Round each number to the nearest ten or hundred.

Nearest 10		Nearest 10		Nearest 100	
8	10	634	630	27	0
47	50	821	820	590	600
81	80	405	410	804	800
74	70	257	260	682	700
59	60	783	780	359	400

Lesson 105

Estimation Practice

Estimate each sum or difference by rounding to the greatest place value.

31 → 30
+ 77 → + 80
estimate: 110

68 → 70
- 52 → - 50
estimate: 20

426 → 400
+ 570 → + 600
estimate: 1000

64 → 60
- 29 → - 30
estimate: 30

57 → 60
+ 84 → + 80
estimate: 140

805 → 800
- 768 → - 800
estimate: 0

539 → 500
+ 185 → + 200
estimate: 700

4165 → 4000
+ 3803 → + 4000
estimate: 8000

742 → 700
- 596 → - 600
estimate: 100

5385 → 5000
+ 1709 → + 2000
estimate: 7000

637 → 600
+ 581 → + 600
estimate: 1200

6540 → 7000
- 2713 → - 3000
estimate: 4000

Lesson 106+

Multiplication Chart

From **Day 106** to **Day 150**, fill in the multiplication chart below as you learn new multiplication facts. Use this worksheet to review and practice.

X	0	1	2	3	4	5	6	7	8	9
0	0	0	0	0	0	0	0	0	0	0
1	0	1	2	3	4	5	6	7	8	9
2	0	2	4	6	8	10	12	14	16	18
3	0	3	6	9	12	15	18	21	24	27
4	0	4	8	12	16	20	24	28	32	36
5	0	5	10	15	20	25	30	35	40	45
6	0	6	12	18	24	30	36	42	48	54
7	0	7	14	21	28	35	42	49	56	63
8	0	8	16	24	32	40	48	56	64	72
9	0	9	18	27	36	45	54	63	72	81

Lesson 106

Understanding Multiplication

A. Fill in the blanks to find the total number of dots.

The total number of dots is:
2 + 2 + 2 = 6

How many dots per die? 2
How many dice? 3

You can write this as:
2 x 3 = 6

B. For each repeated addition, write a multiplication sentence and solve.

4 + 4 + 4 = 4 x 3 = 12

3 + 3 + 3 + 3 = 3 x 4 = 12

5 + 5 + 5 = 5 x 3 = 15

1 + 1 + 1 + 1 = 1 x 4 = 4

0 + 0 + 0 = 0 x 3 = 0

C. Fill in the 0s row and 0s column of the Multiplication Chart on **Day 106+**.
D. Fill in the 1s row and 1s column of the multiplication Chart on **Day 106+**.

Lesson 107

Understanding Multiplication

A. For each repeated addition, fill in the boxes.

Repeated Addition	Groups	Factors	Product
2 + 2 + 2	** ** **	2 x 3	6
4 + 4	**** ****	4 x 2	8
3 + 3 + 3	*** *** ***	3 x 3	9
5 + 5	***** *****	5 x 2	10
4 + 4 + 4	**** **** ****	4 x 3	12

B. For each multiplication, fill in the boxes.

Factors	Array	Commutative Property	Product
2 x 3	⋮ ⋮ ⋮	3 x 2	6
4 x 2	::::	2 x 4	8
5 x 2	:::::	2 x 5	10
5 x 3	::::: ::::: :::::	3 x 5	15

Lesson 108

Multiplying by 10 and 9

A. Let's practice multiplying by 10. Here's the quick way to multiply by 10:

When you multiply by 10, just add 0 to the end.

3 x 10 = 30   140 x 10 = 1400
4 x 10 = 40   295 x 10 = 2950
78 x 10 = 780   500 x 10 = 5000
53 x 10 = 530   628 x 10 = 6280

B. Let's practice multiplying a single digit number times 9. Here's the quick way:

First, subtract 1 from the number multiplied by 9 to get the tens digit.
Second, subtract this tens digit from 9 to get the ones digit.

First, 4 - 1 = 3   Second, 9 - 3 = 6

4 x 9 = 36   9 x 9 = 81
9 x 8 = 72   5 x 9 = 45
7 x 9 = 63   9 x 2 = 18
3 x 9 = 27   6 x 9 = 54

Lesson 109

Multiplication & Counting Money

A. Let's practice multiplying by 0 and 1.

$8 \times 0 = 0$ $7 \times 1 = 7$

$1 \times 6 = 6$ $3 \times 0 = 0$

$0 \times 9 = 0$ $1 \times 5 = 5$

B. For each multiplication, fill in the blanks.

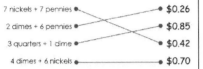

$2 \times 4 = $ ** ** ** ** $= 4 \times 2 = 8$

$5 \times 3 = $ ***** ***** ***** $= 3 \times 5 = 15$

$3 \times 4 = $ *** *** *** *** $= 4 \times 3 = 12$

$8 \times 2 = $ ******** ******** $= 2 \times 8 = 16$

C. Draw lines to match the same amounts.

7 nickels + 7 pennies • • $0.26

2 dimes + 6 pennies • • $0.85

3 quarters + 1 dime • • $0.42

4 dimes + 6 nickels • • $0.70

Lesson 110

Multiplying by 5 & Elapsed Time

A. Let's practice multiplying by 5. Here's the quick way to multiply by 5:

To multiply 5 by an even number:
The tens digit is half the number. The ones digit is 0.

To multiply 5 by an odd number:
Subtract 1 from the number and half the answer to get the tens digit.
The ones digit is 5.

Half of 4 = 2 → $5 \times 4 = 20$ 7 - 1 = 6, Half of 6 = 3 → $7 \times 5 = 35$

$8 \times 5 = 40$ $5 \times 3 = 15$

$5 \times 6 = 30$ $9 \times 5 = 45$

B. Complete the table by finding the time.

Start Time	Elapsed Time	End Time
5:35 A.M.	2 hours 45 minutes	8:20 A.M.
7:20 A.M.	7 hours 5 minutes	2:25 P.M.
9:40 A.M.	7 hours 25 minutes	5:05 P.M.
11:55 A.M.	3 hours 15 minutes	3:10 P.M.

Lesson 113

Multiplying by 2 & Dividing by 2

A. Multiplying by 2 is doubling the number. Let's practice multiplying by 2.

6	2	3	2	0	8	2	2
×2	×9	×2	×5	×2	×2	×4	×7
12	18	6	10	0	16	8	14

B. Dividing by 2 is cutting in half. It's doing the opposite of doubling or multiplying by 2. Let's practice dividing by 2.

$2 \times 2 = 4$ ● ●   ● ●
If I gave you 2 balls, 2 times, you would have 4 balls.

$4 \div 2 = 2$ (● ●) (● ●)
Divide 4 balls into 2 groups. How many are in each group?

$3 \times 2 = 6$ ● ● ●   ● ● ●
$6 \div 2 = 3$ (● ● ●) (● ● ●)
Draw circles to make 2 groups of balls.

$8 \div 2 = 4$ $10 \div 2 = 5$
$12 \div 2 = 6$ $14 \div 2 = 7$
$16 \div 2 = 8$ $18 \div 2 = 9$

Lesson 114

Dividing with 0 and 1 & Perimeters

A. For each problem, fill in the blank and write a division sentence.

If you divide 4 candies into 1 group,
that group will have 4 candies. $4 \div 1 = 4$

If you divide 0 candies into 5 groups,
each group will have 0 candies. $0 \div 5 = 0$

B. Let's practice dividing with 0 and 1. Like subtraction, you can't switch the numbers in division. It only works one direction.

$0 \div 8 = 0$ $7 \div 1 = 7$
$0 \div 3 = 0$ $6 \div 1 = 6$
$5 \div 1 = 5$ $0 \div 7 = 0$
$8 \div 1 = 8$ $4 \div 1 = 4$

C. Calculate the perimeter of each rectangle.

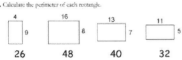

26   48   40   32

Lesson 115

Multiplication, Subtraction & Symmetry

A. Let's practice multiplying by 0, 1, and 2.

0	2	5	2	0	7	2	8
×3	×2	×1	×6	×2	×1	×4	×2
0	4	5	12	0	7	8	16

5	0	9	2	0	7	4	2
×2	×6	×2	×1	×8	×2	×1	×3
10	0	18	2	0	14	4	6

B. Solve the 2-digit subtraction problems.

48	73	65	94	85	70
- 26	- 38	- 49	- 38	- 52	- 46
22	35	16	56	33	24

C. Draw a line of symmetry on each shape.

E   A   C   H

Lesson 116+

Fractions and Decimals

Fractions, decimals, and money are closely related. Complete the table.

Fraction	Decimal	Money	
$15/100$	0.15	15¢ or	$0.15
$53/100$	0.53	53¢ or	$0.53
$29/100$	0.29	29¢ or	$0.29
$98/100$	0.98	98¢ or	$0.98
$60/100$	0.60	60¢ or	$0.60
$46/100$	0.46	46¢ or	$0.46
$25/100$	0.25	25¢ or	$0.25
$72/100$	0.72	72¢ or	$0.72
$31/100$	0.31	31¢ or	$0.31

Lesson 116

Fractions and Decimals

Fractions, decimals and money are closely related. Complete the table.

Fraction	Decimal	Money	
$15/100$	0.15	15¢ or	$0.15
$53/100$	0.53	53¢ or	$0.53
$29/100$	0.29	29¢ or	$0.29
$98/100$	0.98	98¢ or	$0.98
$60/100$	0.60	60¢ or	$0.60
$46/100$	0.46	46¢ or	$0.46
$25/100$	0.25	25¢ or	$0.25
$72/100$	0.72	72¢ or	$0.72
$31/100$	0.31	31¢ or	$0.31

Lesson 117

Modeling Decimals

Write a decimal for each shaded part.

0.35   0.57   0.82

0.43   0.71   0.29

0.2   0.6   0.9

Lesson 118

Money as Decimals

Write the money amounts as decimals.

Seven cents $0.07   Three dollars $3.00
Fourteen cents $0.14   Fifteen dollars $15.00
Forty-two cents $0.42   Eighty dollars $80.00

Two dollars, ten cents $2.10
Thirteen dollars, eight cents $13.08
Sixteen dollars, eleven cents $16.11
Twelve dollars, sixty-one cents $12.61
Twenty-five dollars, twenty cents $25.20
Thirty-nine dollars, seventeen cents $39.17
Seventy-six dollars, ninety-nine cents $76.99
Eighty-four dollars, twenty-four cents $84.24
Ninety-seven dollars, thirty-six cents $97.36

Lesson 119

Adding Decimals

Add the decimals. To add decimals:

First, line up the decimal points.
Second, add the numbers as you would add whole numbers.
Third, carry the decimal point directly down into your answer.

¹ 2.4 + 3.8 **6.2**	¹ 3.5 + 4.9 **8.4**	6.7 + 1.8 **8.5**	9.4 + 2.2 **11.6**	¹ 5.8 + 7.5 **13.3**

2.26 + 8.34 **10.60**	2.63 + 4.86 **7.49**	4.32 + 2.55 **6.87**	6.84 + 6.17 **13.01**

2.37 + 3.96 **6.33**	1.63 + 9.82 **11.45**	9.34 + 7.46 **16.80**	7.65 + 2.59 **10.24**

Lesson 120

Subtracting Decimals

Subtract the decimals. To subtract decimals:

First, line up the decimal points.
Second, subtract the numbers as you would subtract whole numbers.
Third, carry the decimal point directly down into your answer.

⁴ ¹³ 5.3 – 4.8 **0.5**	6.5 – 4.9 **1.6**	7.8 – 3.5 **4.3**	8.3 – 5.6 **2.7**	4.2 – 3.9 **0.3**

5.96 – 5.42 **0.54**	7.23 – 5.63 **1.60**	8.40 – 6.76 **1.64**	9.99 – 4.32 **5.67**

9.46 – 9.35 **0.11**	8.32 – 4.97 **3.35**	7.42 – 6.48 **0.94**	9.71 – 2.75 **6.96**

Lesson 121+

Daily Practice for the Week

From **Day 121** to **Day 125**, solve one row of problems each day.

3 x7 21	4 x2 8	2 x8 16	5 x3 15	3 x6 18	2 x9 18	3 x2 6	1 x3 3
3 x8 24	4 x3 12	3 x6 18	3 x7 21	2 x5 10	9 x2 18	7 x2 14	2 x3 6
3 x9 27	2 x7 14	3 x5 15	2 x8 16	1 x2 2	3 x7 21	2 x2 4	8 x3 24
3 x5 15	2 x3 6	2 x1 2	7 x3 21	6 x3 18	2 x6 12	9 x3 27	2 x5 10
4 x4 16	3 x9 27	2 x5 10	3 x8 24	2 x2 4	2 x4 8	4 x3 12	6 x2 12

Lesson 121

Adding Money & Fractions

A. Look at the menu and answer the questions.

Burger	Hotdog	Drink	Apple	Cookie
$0.55	$0.40	$0.28	$0.15	$0.10

Mark bought a burger and an apple. How much did he spend in all?

$0.70

0.55
+ 0.15
0.70

Emma has 3 nickels and wants to spend all. Which item can she buy?

Apple

Daniel bought a hotdog and drink. How much did he spend in all?

$0.68

0.40
+ 0.28
0.68

Sam has 2 quarters. Which 2 items can he buy without change?

Hotdog, Cookie

B. Color in the shape to show the fraction.

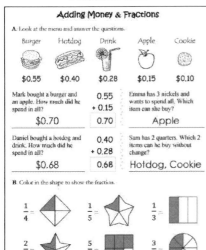

$\frac{1}{4}$ = $\frac{1}{5}$ = $\frac{1}{3}$ =

$\frac{2}{5}$ = $\frac{5}{6}$ = $\frac{3}{8}$ =

Lesson 122

Adding Money

A. Solve the money addition problems.

$2.83 + $6.47 **$9.30**	$4.95 + $8.34 **$13.29**	$2.38 + $3.42 **$5.80**	$8.65 + $7.29 **$15.94**
$7.24 + $2.54 **$9.78**	$9.88 + $7.15 **$17.03**	$4.73 + $5.85 **$10.58**	$3.42 + $7.23 **$10.65**
$6.70 + $6.58 **$13.28**	$8.24 + $3.36 **$11.60**	$2.49 + $5.26 **$7.75**	$7.54 + $1.58 **$9.12**

B. Can you solve this money puzzle? Place a coin in each square so that the total at the end of each row and column is correct.

			31¢
			21¢
35¢	11¢	6¢	

Lesson 123

Money Word Problems

Solve each word problem. Use the space on the right for your work area.

After buying some cookies for $5.00, Dan has $2.50 left. How much money did Dan have to begin with?

$7.50

$5.00 + $2.50 = $7.50

After buying some pencils for $4.75, Rick has $6.50 left. How much money did Rick have to begin with?

$11.25

$4.75 + $6.50 = $11.25

Henry gives $5.75 to Anne. If Henry started with $8.00, how much money does he have left?

$2.25

$8.00 – $5.75 = $2.25

After buying some cards for $4.50, Alice has $3.75 left. How much money did Alice have to begin with?

$8.25

$4.50 + $3.75 = $8.25

Will has $6.50 and Orson has $5.25. How much more money does Will have than Orson?

$1.25

$6.50 – $5.25 = $1.25

Lesson 124

Adding and Subtracting Money

Solve the money addition and subtraction problems.

$95.63 + $32.05 **$127.68**	$82.28 + $63.47 **$145.75**	$49.38 + $45.49 **$94.87**	$38.68 + $48.52 **$87.20**

$86.87 – $34.42 **$52.45**	$83.63 – $35.29 **$48.34**	$60.34 – $36.07 **$24.27**	$74.30 – $57.85 **$16.45**

You can add and subtract money in different currencies such as pounds, euros, yens, peso, or rands in the same way you add and subtract dollars and cents.

£29.84 + £61.65 **£91.49**	€62.48 – €34.36 **€28.12**	¥75.54 + ¥74.56 **¥150.10**	R73.57 – R26.77 **R46.80**

Lesson 125

Adding and Subtracting Money

Solve the money addition and subtraction problems.

$52.65 + $55.87 **$108.52**	$38.75 + $62.80 **$101.55**	$54.97 + $78.83 **$133.80**	$49.42 + $23.67 **$73.09**

$82.50 – $56.56 **$25.94**	$68.20 – $23.94 **$44.26**	$98.38 – $47.59 **$50.79**	$72.42 – $38.72 **$33.70**

£62.54 + £63.64 **£126.18**	€57.43 – €23.69 **€33.74**	₱62.89 + ₱50.87 **₱113.76**	R33.55 – R15.70 **R17.85**

Lesson 126+

Daily Practice for the Week

From **Day 126** to **Day 130**, solve one row of problems each day.

4 x5 20	2 x7 14	8 x3 24	4 x4 16	2 x5 10	3 x4 12	2 x2 4	3 x9 27
4 x6 24	2 x1 2	3 x4 12	2 x6 12	8 x3 24	5 x4 20	3 x2 6	7 x2 14
4 x7 28	5 x2 10	3 x9 27	6 x4 24	3 x3 9	2 x8 16	3 x7 21	4 x2 8
4 x8 32	2 x2 4	6 x3 18	4 x4 16	3 x3 9	2 x9 18	4 x2 8	7 x4 28
4 x9 36	5 x2 10	3 x5 15	3 x6 18	2 x3 6	4 x8 32	3 x9 27	8 x2 16

Lesson 126

Word Problems

Solve each word problem. Use the space on the right for your work area.

Mark solved 36 math problems. Sam solved 28 more problems than Mark. How many problems did Sam solve?

$36 + 28 = 64$

64 problems

Bill had forty-two marbles. Bill gave twenty-eight of his marbles to Ethan. How many marbles does Bill have now?

$42 - 28 = 14$

14 marbles

Emma had 35 dimes. Her mom gave her some dimes. Now Emma has 70 dimes. How many dimes did Emma get from her mom?

$70 - 35 = 35$

35 dimes

Jenny picked 50 apples. She gave 25 apples to her friend, Noah. Later, Jenny picked 15 more apples. How many apples does Jenny have now?

$50 - 25 = 25$
$25 + 15 = 40$

40 apples

Larry read 56 pages of his book yesterday. He read 48 pages today. There are 37 pages left now. How many pages were in Larry's book?

$56 + 48 = 104$
$104 + 37 = 141$

141 pages

There were 82 books on the shelf. Orson took 18 books from the shelf. Kate took some books, too. There are 35 books left now. How many books did Kate take?

$82 - 18 = 64$
$64 - 35 = 29$

29 books

Lesson 127

Word Problems

Solve each word problem. Use the space on the right for your work area.

Samantha rode her bike 26 miles this week. She rode 37 miles last week. How many miles did Samantha ride altogether?

$26 + 37 = 63$

63 miles

William has thirty-five marbles. Ethan has twenty-three more marbles than William. How many marbles does Ethan have?

$35 + 23 = 58$

58 marbles

Daniel has seventy-six dimes. Olivia has fifty-four dimes. How many fewer dimes does Olivia have than Daniel?

$76 - 54 = 22$

22 dimes

There were 41 apples in the basket. Derek put 25 apples in the basket. Mia put 12 apples in the basket. How many apples are in the basket now?

$41 + 25 + 12 = 78$

78 apples

Jenny jumped a rope 35 times. Kyle jumped 18 more times than Jenny. Larry jumped 21 fewer times than Kyle. How many times did Larry jump?

$35 + 18 = 53$
$53 - 21 = 32$

32 times

This year Amber planted 18 roses. Dylan planted twice as many roses as Amber. 18 roses have bloomed so far. How many roses have not bloomed yet?

Dylan planted 36.
$18 + 36 = 54$
$54 - 18 = 36$

36 roses

Lesson 128

Subtracting Money

Solve the money subtraction problems.

$3.56	$8.98	$4.36	$4.50
- $1.80	- $5.26	- $0.73	- $0.28
$1.76	**$3.72**	**$3.63**	**$4.22**

$9.24	$8.20	$7.25	$6.07
- $5.58	- $3.64	- $4.53	- $2.44
$3.66	**$4.56**	**$2.72**	**$3.63**

$8.34	$9.30	$6.19	$5.84
- $4.39	- $2.72	- $0.93	- $0.77
$3.95	**$6.58**	**$5.26**	**$5.07**

$9.91	£8.83	€4.67	¥7.40
- $7.64	- £1.60	- €1.80	- ¥2.85
$2.27	**£7.23**	**€2.87**	**¥4.55**

Lesson 129

Word Problems

Solve each word problem. Use the space on the right for your work area.

Angela had 57 math problems to solve. She solved 18 yesterday and 19 today. How many problems does Angela have left to solve?

$18 + 19 = 37$
$57 - 37 = 20$

20 problems

Sam wants to buy three books that cost $15, $11, and $18. He has $25. How much more money does he need to buy the books?

$15 + 11 + 18 = 44$
$44 - 25 = 19$

19 dollars

Ella planted 32 roses, 26 daisies, and 10 violets. 55 of them have bloomed so far. How many flowers have not bloomed yet?

$32 + 26 + 10 = 68$
$68 - 55 = 13$

13 flowers

Jacob has 9 marbles. Eric has 6 more marbles than Jacob. Owen has 8 more marbles than Eric. How many marbles do they have all together?

Jacob 9 + Eric 15 + Owen 23 = 47

47 marbles

Henry rode his bike 7 miles to the library and then 13 miles to the park. Later he came home the same way. How many miles did Henry ride in all?

$7 + 13 = 20$
$20 + 20 = 40$

40 miles

Thomas has $10. Dylan has $2 more than Thomas. Amy has $7 less than Dylan. Jane has $4 more than Amy. How much money do they have all together?

Thomas 10 + Dylan 12 + Amy 5 + Jane 9 = 36

36 dollars

Lesson 130

Estimating Sums & Time to Words

A. Estimate the sums by rounding the numbers to the nearest ten. Solve the actual problems as well. The first one is done for you.

$35 →$	40	$37 →$	40	$82 →$	80
$+ 54 →$	$+ 50$	$+ 24 →$	$+ 20$	$+ 54 →$	$+ 50$
89	**90**	**61**	**60**	**136**	**130**

$13 →$	10	$87 →$	90	$61 →$	60
$+ 59 →$	$+ 60$	$+ 43 →$	$+ 40$	$+ 24 →$	$+ 20$
72	**70**	**130**	**130**	**85**	**80**

$76 →$	80	$38 →$	40	$95 →$	100
$+ 73 →$	$+ 70$	$+ 46 →$	$+ 50$	$+ 76 →$	$+ 80$
149	**150**	**84**	**90**	**171**	**180**

B. Write each time in digital form.

ten to three	2:50	quarter to nine	8:45
half past two	2:30	quarter past five	5:15
five after one	1:05	ten after eleven	11:10
ten after six	6:10	twenty to eight	7:40

Lesson 131+

Daily Practice for the Week

From **Day 131** to **Day 135**, solve one row of problems each day.

4	7	3	5	6	4	4	1
x 9	x 3	x 4	x 2	x 3	x 4	x 8	x 3
36	**21**	**12**	**10**	**18**	**16**	**32**	**3**

5	2	4	2	9	3	4	3
x 5	x 9	x 7	x 5	x 4	x 6	x 2	x 9
25	**18**	**28**	**10**	**36**	**18**	**8**	**27**

5	2	3	5	1	2	5	6
x 6	x 3	x 3	x 4	x 9	x 5	x 8	x 4
30	**6**	**15**	**4**	**18**	**25**	**16**	**24**

5	2	3	6	3	2	4	3
x 7	x 2	x 4	x 5	x 3	x 7	x 5	x 9
35	**4**	**12**	**30**	**9**	**14**	**20**	**27**

5	2	3	4	2	2	5	3
x 8	x 6	x 9	x 4	x 1	x 8	x 5	x 2
40	**12**	**27**	**16**	**2**	**16**	**35**	**6**

Lesson 131

Let's Review!

A. Follow the instructions using **My 100s Chart** on page 9.

✓ Describe the relationship between skip counting and multiplication.

Every number you circled is an answer to a multiplication problem.

B. Look at the diagram and answer the question.

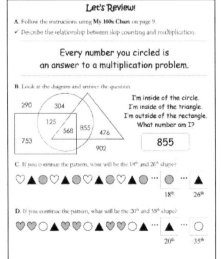

290, 304, 125, 568, 855, 476, 753, 902

I'm inside of the circle.
I'm inside of the triangle.
I'm outside of the rectangle.
What number am I?

855

C. If you continue the pattern, what will be the 18th and 26th shape?

♡ ▲ ● ♡ ▲ ● ♡ ▲ ● ♡ ▲ ● ⋯ ● ⋯ ▲

18th   26th

D. If you continue the pattern, what will be the 20th and 35th shape?

♡ ♡ ○ ▲ ♡ ♡ ○ ▲ ♡ ♡ ○ ▲ ⋯ ▲ ⋯ ○

20th   35th

Lesson 132

Let's Review!

A. Solve the addition problems.

25	350	122	529	349
+ 55	+ 260	+ 357	+ 312	+ 324
80	**610**	**479**	**841**	**673**

B. Color one-half of each shape with your favorite color!

C. Solve the word problem. Use the space on the right for your work area.

A tree has four branches.
Each branch has two nests.
Each nest has five eggs.
How many eggs are there in all?

There are 4 x 2 nests.
8 nests x 5 eggs = 40

40 eggs

Lesson 133

Let's Review!

A. Write multiplication facts for the array of dots.

$2 \times 3 = 6$	$3 \times 2 = 6$
$2 \times 5 = 10$	$5 \times 2 = 10$
$3 \times 4 = 12$	$4 \times 3 = 12$
$3 \times 5 = 15$	$5 \times 3 = 15$

B. Solve each money word problem. Write the amount in cents.

Henry has 4 dimes, 5 nickels, and 7 pennies. How much money does Henry have in all?

72 ¢

Orson has 2 quarters, 2 dimes, 3 nickels, and 4 pennies. How much money does Orson have in all?

89 ¢

Jacob bought four stickers. Each sticker costs 14¢. How much money did Jacob spend in all?

56 ¢

C. Put each number into the appropriate space of the Venn diagram.

12 88
67 45

Even / Less than 50

88   12   45   67

Lesson 134

Let's Review! I

A. The tables show how much of each ingredient you need to make treat bags. Complete all the tables. Use **My 100s Chart** on page 9 to help you.

One Treat Bag
- 12 peanuts
- 4 candies
- 8 pretzels
- 15 raisins

Two Treat Bags	Five Treat Bags	Ten Treat Bags
24 peanuts	60 peanuts	120 peanuts
8 candies	20 candies	40 candies
16 pretzels	40 pretzels	80 pretzels
30 raisins	75 raisins	150 raisins

B. Complete the next worksheet, too.

Lesson 134

Let's Review! II

B. The tally chart shows the number of coins collected by five children.

Barry	Nina	Carol	Matt	Wade

✓ List the children in order from smallest to largest coin collection.

Matt < Nina < Barry < Wade < Carol

✓ Wade, Matt, and Barry have 53 coins together.

✓ Wade has 11 more coins than Matt and 16 fewer coins than Carol.

✓ If Carol gives 15 coins to Nina, Carol will have 23 coins.

C. Look at the price of each item and answer the questions.

School Supplies
- Pencil - 8¢
- Paper - 25¢
- Eraser - 7¢
- Folder - 17¢
- Tape - 20¢

Kate bought one tape and one folder. How much did she spend in all? — 37 ¢

How much would one pencil, one folder, and one eraser cost? — 32 ¢

Eric spent 14¢. What did he buy? — 2 erasers

Justin has 65¢. He buys two items and gets 20¢ change. What does he buy? — paper, tape

Laura spent 40¢ on three items. What did she buy? — pencil, paper, eraser

Lesson 135

Subtraction Practice

A. Complete the subtraction problems.

$8 - 3 = 5$ $10 - 7 = 3$

$9 - 3 = 6$ $12 - 5 = 7$

$10 - 3 = 7$ $14 - 9 = 5$

$7 - 7 = 0$ $20 - 10 = 10$

$9 - 8 = 1$ $40 - 10 = 30$

$10 - 7 = 3$ $50 - 10 = 40$

15	20	23	40	48	37
- 11	- 11	- 15	- 23	- 33	- 21
4	9	8	17	15	16

13	16	17	23	33	43
- 9	- 8	- 10	- 19	- 29	- 39
4	8	7	4	4	4

B. Count by 3s to fill in the blanks.

3, 6, 9, 12, 15, 18, 21, 24, 27, 30

Lesson 136+

Daily Practice for the Week

From **Day 136** to **Day 140**, solve one row of problems each day.

5 x9	2 x7	4 x8	3 x7	5 x5	3 x4	6 x2	8 x5
45	14	32	21	25	12	12	40

5 x6	8 x3	3 x6	5 x4	4 x9	2 x5	6 x2	4 x4
30	24	18	20	36	10	12	16

6 x6	2 x5	3 x4	5 x7	3 x9	5 x8	4 x6	5 x5
36	10	12	35	27	40	24	25

6 x7	3 x5	5 x6	2 x9	7 x3	4 x8	2 x2	8 x5
42	15	30	18	21	32	4	40

6 x8	2 x4	5 x9	3 x3	4 x5	3 x7	6 x6	7 x4
48	8	45	9	20	21	36	28

Lesson 136

Let's Review!

A. Complete the addition and subtraction problems.

$8 + 5 = 13$ $124 + 48 = 172$

$14 - 7 = 7$ $218 + 67 = 285$

B. Solve the problems and fill in the blanks.

✓ How many tens are in 273? — 7

✓ What time is 4 hours and 20 minutes **before** 11:40? — 7:20

✓ What is the greatest number of coins you need to make 40¢ without using pennies? — 8 nickels

✓ If you put 5 apples in one basket, how many baskets do you need to put 40 apples? — 8 baskets

C. Draw the other half of each shape to make it symmetrical.

D. Count by 4s to fill in the blanks.

4, 8, 12, 16, 20, 24, 28, 32, 36, 40

E. East-west highways have even numbers. North-south highways have odd numbers.

Lesson 137

Let's Review!

A. Complete the addition and subtraction squares.

+	10	20	30	40
9	19	29	39	49
10	20	30	40	50
18	28	38	48	58

-	5	7	9	10
11	6	4	2	1
15	10	8	6	5
18	13	11	9	8

B. Count by 10s and label the dots.

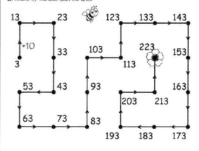

Lesson 138

Let's Review!

A. Solve the addition and subtraction problems.

800	642	402	600	3945
- 135	- 256	- 175	- 258	+ 2526
665	386	227	342	6471

B. Write the fractions in order from largest to smallest.

$$\frac{2}{6} \quad \frac{2}{4} \quad \frac{2}{3} \quad \frac{2}{8} \quad \Rightarrow \quad \frac{2}{3} > \frac{2}{4} > \frac{2}{6} > \frac{2}{8}$$

C. Solve the problems and fill in the blanks.

✓ What time is fifty minutes **after** 9:20? — 10:10

✓ 16 hundreds + 18 tens + 15 ones — 1795

✓ Ron bought 5 candies at 6¢ each and 4 lollipops at 8¢ each. He paid with $1. How much change did he get? — 38¢

✓ There are 5 chickens, 7 geese, and 8 ducks. How many legs are there on all the animals? — 40 legs

✓ One school year is 180 days. If you don't repeat or skip a grade, how many days will it take to complete EP Math 1 through EP Math 4? (You may use a calculator.) — 720 days

Lesson 139

Let's Review!

A. Complete the problems. Use the space on the right for your work area.

65	956	$7.53	438
+ 85	+ 347	- $2.38	+ 38
150	1303	$5.15	476

B. Compare the amounts of money using <, >, or =.

4 dollars + 2 nickels + 3 pennies ⊙< 425¢

C. Compare the fractions using >, <, or =.

$$\frac{2}{3} > \frac{2}{6} \qquad \frac{1}{2} > \frac{1}{4} \qquad \frac{3}{4} > \frac{3}{8}$$

D. Solve the problems and fill in the blanks.

✓ What time is thirty minutes **after** 12:50? — 1:20

✓ 5 thousands + 14 hundreds + 18 tens + 12 ones — 6592

✓ Ladybugs have six legs. How many legs would be on seven ladybugs? — 42 legs

E. Count by 5s to fill in the blanks.

5, 10, 15, 20, 25, 30, 35, 40, 45, 50

Lesson 140

Subtracting with Zeros

Let's practice subtracting with zeros.

$\overset{4\ 10\ 10}{5\ 0\ 0}$	$\overset{6\ 10\ 10}{7\ 0\ 0}$	$\overset{7\ 1\ 10}{8\ 2\ 0}$	$\overset{3\ 10}{4\ 0\ 0}$
- 2 4 4	- 5 5 6	- 4 6 8	- 3 2 0
2 5 6	1 4 4	3 5 2	8 0

$\overset{4\ 10\ 10}{5\ 0\ 0}$	$\overset{7\ 10}{8\ 1\ 0}$	$\overset{8\ 10\ 10}{9\ 0\ 0}$	$\overset{2\ 10\ 12}{3\ 0\ 2}$
- 3 3 1	- 6 9 5	- 4 8 3	- 2 8 5
1 6 9	1 1 5	4 1 7	1 7

$\overset{11\ 1\ 10}{7\ 2\ 0}$	$\overset{4\ 10\ 10}{5\ 0\ 0}$	$\overset{5\ 10\ 13}{6\ 0\ 3}$	$\overset{6\ 10\ 10}{7\ 0\ 0}$
- 5 6 8	- 3 2 2	- 2 2 9	- 4 0 7
1 5 2	1 7 8	3 7 4	2 9 3

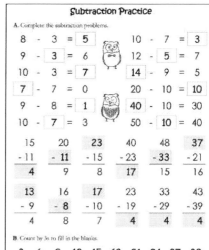

Lesson 141+

Daily Practice for the Week

From **Day 141** to **Day 145**, solve one row of problems each day.

6 ×9	5 ×4	2 ×6	3 ×4	7 ×6	2 ×2	2 ×7	3 ×3
54	**20**	**12**	**12**	**42**	**4**	**14**	**9**
5 ×9	4 ×4	3 ×7	1 ×7	5 ×5	6 ×3	5 ×7	8 ×6
45	**16**	**21**	**7**	**25**	**18**	**35**	**48**
7 ×7	4 ×9	6 ×4	5 ×8	6 ×9	4 ×2	3 ×9	7 ×4
49	**36**	**24**	**40**	**54**	**8**	**27**	**28**
7 ×8	3 ×2	5 ×7	6 ×1	2 ×5	4 ×8	2 ×9	5 ×6
56	**6**	**35**	**6**	**10**	**32**	**18**	**30**
7 ×9	5 ×3	2 ×8	6 ×7	4 ×5	5 ×9	6 ×6	3 ×8
63	**15**	**16**	**42**	**20**	**45**	**36**	**24**

Lesson 141

Comparing Money & Decimals and Fractions

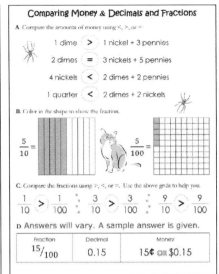

A. Compare the amounts of money using <, >, or =

1 dime **>** 1 nickel + 3 pennies

2 dimes **=** 3 nickels + 5 pennies

4 nickels **<** 2 dimes + 2 pennies

1 quarter **<** 2 dimes + 2 nickels

B. Color in the shape to show the fraction.

$\frac{5}{10}$ = $\frac{5}{100}$ =

C. Compare the fractions using >, <, or =. Use the above grids to help you.

$\frac{1}{10}$ **>** $\frac{1}{100}$ $\frac{3}{10}$ **>** $\frac{3}{100}$ $\frac{9}{10}$ **>** $\frac{9}{100}$

D. Answers will vary. A sample answer is given.

Fraction	Decimal	Money
$\frac{15}{100}$	0.15	15¢ or $0.15

Lesson 142

Comparing Money & Decimals and Fractions

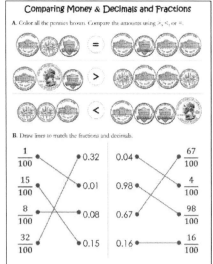

A. Color all the pennies brown. Compare the amounts using >, <, or =.

(row 1) **=**

(row 2) **>**

(row 3) **<**

B. Draw lines to match the fractions and decimals.

$\frac{1}{100}$ • → • 0.32   0.04 • → • $\frac{67}{100}$

$\frac{15}{100}$ • → • 0.01   0.98 • → • $\frac{4}{100}$

$\frac{8}{100}$ • → • 0.08   0.67 • → • $\frac{98}{100}$

$\frac{32}{100}$ • → • 0.15   0.16 • → • $\frac{16}{100}$

Lesson 143

Comparing Money & Decimals and Fractions

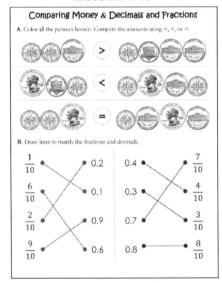

A. Color all the pennies brown. Compare the amounts using >, <, or =.

(row 1) **>**

(row 2) **<**

(row 3) **=**

B. Draw lines to match the fractions and decimals.

$\frac{1}{10}$ • → • 0.2   0.4 • → • $\frac{7}{10}$

$\frac{6}{10}$ • → • 0.1   0.3 • → • $\frac{4}{10}$

$\frac{2}{10}$ • → • 0.9   0.7 • → • $\frac{3}{10}$

$\frac{9}{10}$ • → • 0.6   0.8 • → • $\frac{8}{10}$

Lesson 144

Comparing Money & Decimals and Fractions

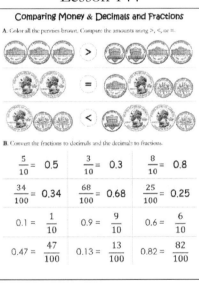

A. Color all the pennies brown. Compare the amounts using >, <, or =.

(row 1) **>**

(row 2) **=**

(row 3) **<**

B. Convert the fractions to decimals and the decimals to fractions.

$\frac{5}{10}$ = 0.5 $\frac{3}{10}$ = 0.3 $\frac{8}{10}$ = 0.8

$\frac{34}{100}$ = 0.34 $\frac{68}{100}$ = 0.68 $\frac{25}{100}$ = 0.25

0.1 = $\frac{1}{10}$ 0.9 = $\frac{9}{10}$ 0.6 = $\frac{6}{10}$

0.47 = $\frac{47}{100}$ 0.13 = $\frac{13}{100}$ 0.82 = $\frac{82}{100}$

Lesson 145

Decimals and Fractions

A. Color in the shape to show the fraction.

$\frac{3}{10}$ = $\frac{78}{100}$ =

B. Compare the fractions using >, <, or =. Use above grids to help you.

$\frac{2}{10}$ **>** $\frac{2}{100}$ $\frac{4}{10}$ **>** $\frac{4}{100}$ $\frac{6}{10}$ **>** $\frac{6}{100}$

$\frac{3}{10}$ **<** $\frac{78}{100}$ $\frac{8}{10}$ **>** $\frac{25}{100}$ $\frac{4}{10}$ **=** $\frac{40}{100}$

C. Compare the decimals using >, <, or =.

0.7 **>** 0.2   0.5 **<** 0.7   0.6 **>** 0.4

0.1 **<** 0.6   0.9 **=** 0.9   0.3 **>** 0.2

0.4 **<** 0.9   0.5 **>** 0.1   0.4 **<** 0.7

0.3 **=** 0.3   0.2 **<** 0.8   0.8 **>** 0.5

Lesson 146+

Daily Practice for the Week

From **Day 146** to **Day 150**, solve one row of problems each day.

7 ×9	8 ×4	6 ×6	3 ×5	9 ×5	4 ×2	5 ×7	6 ×8
63	**32**	**36**	**15**	**45**	**8**	**35**	**48**
8 ×8	5 ×2	3 ×7	0 ×2	2 ×6	7 ×8	9 ×4	5 ×6
64	**10**	**21**	**0**	**12**	**56**	**36**	**30**
8 ×9	3 ×6	4 ×9	7 ×6	5 ×8	6 ×1	7 ×2	6 ×9
72	**18**	**36**	**42**	**40**	**6**	**14**	**54**
9 ×9	2 ×6	4 ×7	5 ×3	9 ×2	8 ×6	5 ×5	3 ×8
81	**12**	**28**	**15**	**18**	**48**	**25**	**24**
8 ×2	4 ×5	3 ×9	6 ×7	1 ×8	4 ×6	5 ×9	7 ×8
16	**20**	**27**	**42**	**8**	**24**	**45**	**56**

Lesson 146

Comparing Decimals & Adding 2-Digits

A. Compare the decimals using <, >, or =

0.02 **<** 0.08   0.03 **<** 0.5

0.05 **>** 0.01   0.09 **<** 0.7

0.26 **=** 0.26   0.49 **>** 0.3

0.37 **>** 0.04   0.35 **<** 0.5

0.65 **>** 0.59   0.78 **>** 0.4

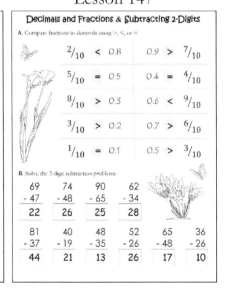

B. Solve the 2-digit addition problems.

46 +85	62 +67	52 +14	64 +79	52 +38	85 +87
131	**129**	**66**	**143**	**90**	**172**

26 +87	39 +36	93 +52	79 +48		
113	**75**	**145**	**127**		

Lesson 147

Decimals and Fractions & Subtracting 2-Digits

A. Compare fractions to decimals using >, <, or =

$\frac{2}{10}$ **<** 0.8   0.9 **>** $\frac{7}{10}$

$\frac{5}{10}$ **=** 0.5   0.4 **=** $\frac{4}{10}$

$\frac{8}{10}$ **>** 0.3   0.6 **<** $\frac{9}{10}$

$\frac{3}{10}$ **>** 0.2   0.7 **>** $\frac{6}{10}$

$\frac{1}{10}$ **=** 0.1   0.5 **>** $\frac{3}{10}$

B. Solve the 2-digit subtraction problems.

69 -47	74 -48	90 -65	62 -34		
22	**26**	**25**	**28**		

81 -37	40 -19	48 -35	52 -26	65 -48	36 -26
44	**21**	**13**	**26**	**17**	**10**

Lesson 148

Decimals and Fractions & Adding 3-Digits

A. Draw lines to match the fractions and decimals.

$\frac{2}{100}$ •	• 0.12
$\frac{22}{100}$ •	• 0.2
$\frac{2}{10}$ •	• 0.02
$\frac{12}{100}$ •	• 0.22

0.4 •	• $\frac{46}{100}$
0.64 •	• $\frac{4}{10}$
0.6 •	• $\frac{64}{100}$
0.46 •	• $\frac{6}{10}$

B. Solve the 3-digit addition problems.

289	453	832
+ 919	+ 657	+ 128
1208	1110	960

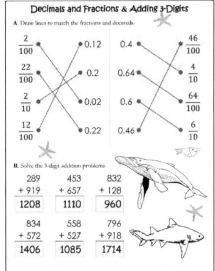

834	558	796
+ 572	+ 527	+ 918
1406	1085	1714

Lesson 149

Hundredths & Subtracting 3-Digits

A. Write a decimal for each shaded part.

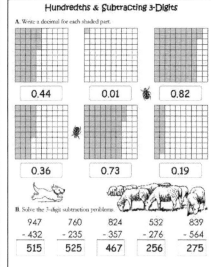

0.44	0.01	0.82

0.36	0.73	0.19

B. Solve the 3-digit subtraction problems.

947	760	824	532	839
- 432	- 235	- 357	- 276	- 564
515	525	467	256	275

Lesson 150

Place Value & Making Change

A. Draw lines to match the numbers with their place value descriptions.

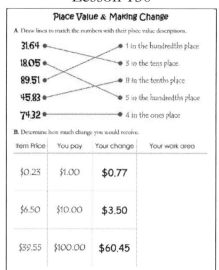

31.64 •	• 1 in the hundredths place
18.05 •	• 3 in the tens place.
89.51 •	• 8 in the tenths place
45.83 •	• 5 in the hundredths place
74.32 •	• 4 in the ones place

B. Determine how much change you would receive.

Item Price	You pay	Your change	Your work area
$0.23	$1.00	$0.77	
$6.50	$10.00	$3.50	
$39.55	$100.00	$60.45	

Lesson 151

Multiplication & Measuring Length

A. Solve the multiplication problems.

3	6	2	4	7	9	1	6
x9	x6	x2	x8	x3	x9	x5	x8
27	36	4	32	21	81	5	48

5	6	8	5	4	3	2	9
x7	x3	x8	x3	x6	x8	x4	x5
35	18	64	15	24	24	8	45

2	7	4	7	8	7	9	5
x6	x9	x4	x7	x2	x4	x1	x5
12	63	16	49	16	28	9	25

B. Match the diamonds on the inch ruler with their positions.

$\frac{1}{2}$ $\frac{7}{8}$ $\frac{1}{4}$ $1\frac{3}{4}$ $2\frac{9}{16}$ $1\frac{3}{8}$ $2\frac{15}{16}$ $2\frac{3}{16}$

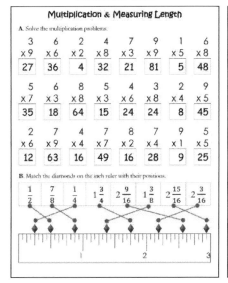

Lesson 152

Fact Families & Measuring Length

A. Use the numbers in the triangles to create fact families.

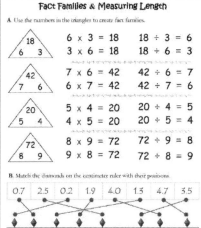

18 / 6 3
6 x 3 = 18   18 ÷ 3 = 6
3 x 6 = 18   18 ÷ 6 = 3

42 / 7 6
7 x 6 = 42   42 ÷ 6 = 7
6 x 7 = 42   42 ÷ 7 = 6

20 / 5 4
5 x 4 = 20   20 ÷ 4 = 5
4 x 5 = 20   20 ÷ 5 = 4

72 / 8 9
8 x 9 = 72   72 ÷ 9 = 8
9 x 8 = 72   72 ÷ 8 = 9

B. Match the diamonds on the centimeter ruler with their positions.

0.7	2.5	0.2	1.9	4.0	1.3	4.7	3.5

Lesson 153

Money Word Problems

A. Look at the price of each item and answer the questions.

Book $3.65	Dictionary $4.80	Puzzle $1.90	Magazine $2.40
Notebook $1.15	Folder $0.75	Bookmark $0.49	Card $1.55

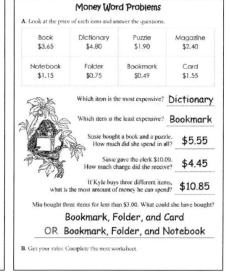

Which item is the most expensive? **Dictionary**

Which item is the least expensive? **Bookmark**

Susie bought a book and a puzzle. How much did she spend in all? **$5.55**

Susie gave the clerk $10.00. How much change did she receive? **$4.45**

If Kyle buys three different items, what is the most amount of money he can spend? **$10.85**

Mia bought three items for less than $3.00. What could she have bought?
Bookmark, Folder, and Card
OR Bookmark, Folder, and Notebook

B. Get your ruler. Complete the next worksheet.

Lesson 154

Perimeter & Units of Weight

A. Roll a die. The first roll is your length. The second roll is your width. Write them down and find the perimeter.

Roll!	Length	Width	Perimeter
Round 1			
Round 2			
Round 3			
Round 4			
Round 5			

B. Draw lines to match the weights in grams and kilograms.

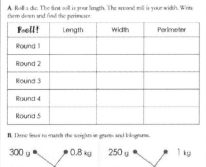

300 g •	• 0.8 kg
200 g •	• 0.3 kg
800 g •	• 0.9 kg
500 g •	• 0.2 kg
900 g •	• 0.5 kg

250 g •	• 1 kg
750 g •	• 0.25 kg
1000 g •	• 1.5 kg
1500 g •	• 4 kg
4000 g •	• 0.75 kg

Lesson 155

Time to Words, Math Terms & Adding Weights

A. Write each time in digital form.

half past nine	9:30	twenty after ten	10:20
ten to seven	6:50	forty past seven	7:40
half to eight	7:30	quarter after two	2:15
five past three	3:05	quarter to eleven	10:45

B. Review **Part A** and **Part B** on **Day 100**. Cover the right column with a piece of paper, and explain what each term means. Provide examples if you can.

C. Look at the weight of each coin and answer the questions.

Penny 3.11 grams	Nickel 5 grams	Dime 2.27 grams	Quarter 5.67 grams

How many grams do a penny and a quarter weigh?	3.11 + 5.67	How many grams do a dime and a nickel weigh?	2.27 + 5.00
8.78 grams	8.78	7.27 grams	7.27

Two coins have a value of 11 cents. How many grams do the coins weigh?	2.27 + 3.11	Two coins have a value of 30 cents. How many grams do the coins weigh?	5.67 + 5.00
5.38 grams	5.38	10.67 grams	10.67

Lesson 156

Fractions & Subtracting Weights

A. Color in the shape to show the fraction.

$\frac{1}{2}$ $\frac{1}{2}$ $\frac{1}{2}$

$\frac{1}{3}$ $\frac{1}{3}$ $\frac{1}{3}$

B. Look at the weight of each coin and answer the questions.

Penny 3.11 grams	Nickel 5 grams	Dime 2.27 grams	Quarter 5.67 grams

How many more grams does a nickel weigh than a penny?	5.00 - 3.11	How many fewer grams does a dime weigh than a quarter?	5.67 - 2.27
1.89 grams	1.89	3.40 grams	3.40

Two coins have a value of 15 cents. What is the weight difference between the two coins?	5.00 - 2.27	Two coins have a value of 26 cents. What is the weight difference between the two coins?	5.67 - 3.11
2.73 grams	2.73	2.56 grams	2.56

Lesson 157

Tally Marks & Reading Scales

A. Five children are playing a game. They record their scores with tally marks.

Kyle	Ron	Jenny	Marie	Sam
卌 卌 卌 卌卌	卌 卌 卌卌‖	卌 卌 卌 卌‖	卌 卌 卌卌‖‖	卌 卌 卌 卌

✓ List the children in order from lowest score to highest score.

Ron < Sam < Kyle < Jenny < Marie

✓ What is the total score of the boys (Kyle, Ron, Sam)? **59**

✓ What is the total score of the girls (Jenny, Marie)? **66**

✓ How many more points did Marie score than Ron? **21**

✓ Sam wants to give his points equally to the other four players. How many points should he give to each person? **5**

B. Match the diamonds on the pound scale with their positions.

Lesson 158

Guessing Weight & Multiplication

A. Estimate the weight of each object and circle your answer.

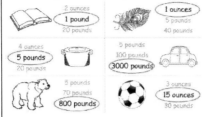

B. The tables show how much of each ingredient you need to make lunch bags. Complete all the tables. Use **My 100s Chart** on page 9 to help you.

One Lunch Bag	Three Lunch Bags	Five Lunch Bags
2 slices bread	6 slices bread	10 slices bread
4 slices ham	12 slices ham	20 slices ham
7 carrot sticks	21 carrot sticks	35 carrot sticks
12 chips	36 chips	60 chips
3 cookies	9 cookies	15 cookies

Lesson 159

Let's Review!

A. Complete the problems.

5000	1000	9	4	7	7
+ 2326	- 400	x 2	x 6	x 5	x 8
7326	600	18	24	35	56

B. Solve the problems and fill in the blanks.

✓ Three thousands, six hundreds, twelve tens, and fourteen ones. **3734**

✓ Mark has $14, two quarters, and two nickels. Ron has $6 and a quarter. How much do they have in all? **$20.85**

✓ John read a book for 25 minutes. After lunch, he read more for 35 minutes. How many hours did he read? **1 hour**

✓ There are two cups in one pint. How many cups are there in five pints? **10 cups**

✓ There are five nickels in one quarter. How many nickels are there in four quarters? **20 nickels**

✓ Henry wants to give 27 stickers equally to his three friends. How many should he give to each friend? **9 stickers**

✓ If you cut a string that is 42 inches long into six equal pieces, how long will each piece be? **7 inches**

C. If you are in America, use the next worksheet to learn units of measurement.

Lesson 160

Let's Review!

A. Complete the problems.

4000	8000	6	4	6	8
+ 350	- 3000	x 3	x 5	x 6	x 9
4350	5000	18	20	36	72

B. Solve the problems and fill in the blanks.

✓ 5 thousands, 15 hundreds, 17 tens, and 4 ones. **6474**

✓ A pencil costs 7¢. How much will six pencils cost? **42¢**

✓ It's fifteen till five. How many minutes past four is it? **45 min.**

✓ Orson bought two books that cost $12 and $23. He paid with $50. How much change did he receive? **$15.00**

✓ Five children want to share 30 marbles equally. How many marbles will each child get? **6 marbles**

B. Draw lines to match the amounts in milliliters and liters.

300 ml	0.7 l	350 ml	1 l
500 ml	0.3 l	1000 ml	0.35 l
700 ml	0.5 l	1750 ml	1.75 l

Lesson 161

Word Problems

Solve each word problem. Use the space on the right for your work area.

Brian has 48 baseball cards. Matt has 35 more baseball cards than Brian. How many baseball cards does Matt have? $48 + 35 = 83$

83 baseball cards

Olivia found 85 berries in the woods. James found 42 berries. How many more berries did Olivia find than James? $85 - 42 = 43$

43 berries

Heather had 80 cents. She spent 28 cents on candies and 32 cents on cookies. How much money does Heather have left? $28 + 32 = 60$ $80 - 60 = 20$

20 cents

Ryan had 26 dimes. His mom gave him some more dimes. Now he has 53 dimes. How many dimes did Ryan get from his mom? $53 - 26 = 27$

27 dimes

There were 65 children in the room. 12 children have left, and then 15 children have entered. How many children are there in the room now? $65 - 12 = 53$ $53 + 15 = 68$

68 children

Julia found 128 seashells on the beach. She put 42 in her bucket and gave some to Terri. She had 26 seashells left. How many seashells did Julia give to Terri? $128 - 42 = 86$ $86 - 26 = 60$

60 seashells

Lesson 162

Word Problems

Solve each word problem. Use the space on the right for your work area.

Ron wants to buy three books that cost $8, $9, and $6. He has saved $15 so far. How much more money does Ron need to buy all three books? $8 + 9 + 6 = 23$ $23 - 15 = 8$

8 dollars

Sam has 10 marbles. Clara has 6 more marbles than Sam. Matt has 8 more marbles than Sam. How many marbles do they have in all? Sam 10 + Clara 16 + Matt 18 = 44

44 marbles

Justin had 18 marbles. He got 7 from Mark and 5 from Owen. Justin gave 20 marbles to Mia. How many marbles does Justin have left? $18 + 7 + 5 = 30$ $30 - 20 = 10$

10 marbles

Julio saved $10 in May. He saved $18 in June and $15 in July. Then Julio spent $28 during summer vacation. How much money does Julio have left? $10 + 18 + 15 = 43$ $43 - 28 = 15$

15 dollars

Abby needs 40 paper cups for her party. She already has 7 red cups, 5 blue cups, and 8 pink cups. How many more cups should Abby buy? $7 + 5 + 8 = 20$ $40 - 20 = 20$

20 paper cups

Ann has 10 books. Ron has 5 more books than Ann. Jane has 4 fewer books than Ron. Leah has 6 more books than Jane. How many books do they have in all? Ann 10 + Ron 15 + Jane 11 + Leah 17 = 53

53 books

Lesson 163

Estimation Practice

A. Estimate each sum or difference by rounding to the greatest place value.

25 → 30	82 → 80	483 → 500
+ 93 → + 90	- 47 → - 50	+ 901 → + 900
estimate: **120**	estimate: **30**	estimate: **1400**

79 → 80	62 → 60	914 → 900
- 51 → - 50	+ 58 → + 60	- 357 → - 400
estimate: **30**	estimate: **120**	estimate: **500**

472 → 500	2613 → 3000
+ 948 → + 900	+ 5453 → + 5000
estimate: **1400**	estimate: **8000**

854 → 900	7358 → 7000
- 206 → - 200	- 5294 → - 5000
estimate: **700**	estimate: **2000**

B. Can you solve this number riddle?

I am a 4-digit number. Three of my digits are zeros. I am the greatest number possible with those characteristics. What number am I? **9000**

Lesson 164

Word Problems

Solve each word problem. Use the space on the right for your work area.

James found 48 berries in the woods. Olivia found 38 berries. How many berries did they find altogether? $48 + 38 = 86$

86 berries

Lucy read 35 pages of the reading assignment. Carrie read 19 more pages than Lucy. How many pages did Carrie read? $35 + 19 = 54$

54 pages

Angela baked 54 cookies for her birthday party. Her family and friends ate 38 of them. How many cookies does Angela have left? $54 - 38 = 16$

16 cookies

Kyle sold 67 cups of lemonade at his stand. Nancy sold only 25 cups at her stand. How many fewer cups of lemonade did Nancy sell? $67 - 25 = 42$

42 cups

Kate picked 13 apples. Mia picked twice as many apples as Kate. They used 15 apples to make a pie. How many apples are left? $13 + 26 = 39$ $39 - 15 = 24$

24 apples

Ron, Matt, Naomi collect stamps. Ron has 34 stamps. Matt has 12 more stamps than Ron. Naomi has 15 fewer stamps than Matt. How many stamps does Naomi have? $34 + 12 = 46$ $46 - 15 = 31$

31 stamps

Lesson 165

Tricky Word Problems

Solve each word problem. Use the space on the right for your work area.

Mark has 8 red marbles and 5 blue marbles. His sister has 6 red marbles. How many marbles does Mark have? $8 + 5 = 13$

13 marbles

There were 5 girls and 14 boys in the gym. 6 boys went outside to run laps. How many boys were in the gym now? $14 - 6 = 8$

8 boys

13 problems were on the test. Terri got 8 problems correctly. Josh got 7 problems correctly. How many problems did Josh do incorrectly? $13 - 7 = 6$

6 problems

Adam picked 10 apples. He gave 4 of them to Thomas and picked 6 more apples. How many apples did Adam pick in total? $10 + 6 = 16$

16 apples

Thomas wants to buy 2 candy bars. Candy bars cost 7 cents each and cookies cost 6 cents each. How much will Thomas pay? $7 \times 2 = 14$

14 cents

Mia spent 9 minutes listening to music. She took a 5 minute snack break. Then she listened for 7 more minutes. How long did Mia listen to music altogether? $9 + 7 = 16$

16 minutes

Lesson 166

Tricky Word Problems

Solve each word problem. Use the space on the right for your work area.

Daniela spent $20 on comic books. She spent $32 on puzzles and $14 on treats. How much more money did Daniela spend on puzzles than treats?

18 dollars $32 - 14 = 18$

At the park, Miguel saw 18 oak trees. He saw 12 birds on one oak tree and 23 birds on another oak tree. How many birds did Miguel see altogether?

35 birds $12 + 23 = 35$

There are 20 children in the book club. Sofia read 26 books last month. Mia read 13 more books than Sofia. How many books did Mia read?

39 books $26 + 13 = 39$

50 pens were in the drawer. 25 pens were red and 23 pens were blue. John took 26 pens from the drawer. How many pens were in the drawer then?

24 pens $50 - 26 = 24$

The auditorium has 95 seats. 42 people sat down to listen to a lecture. 35 people were outside talking to each other. How many seats were empty?

53 seats $95 - 42 = 53$

36 roses bloomed in the garden. There were 25 different types of flowers. Maria picked 13 roses to decorate her room. How many roses were in the garden then?

23 roses $36 - 13 = 23$

Lesson 167

Word Problems

Solve each word problem. Use the space on the right for your work area.

There were 55 paper cups in the cabinet. Lucy took 16 cups from the cabinet. Carlos took 18 cups. How many paper cups were left in the cabinet?

21 paper cups $16 + 18 = 34$ $55 - 34 = 21$

At the garden, Mia planted 35 flowers. Her sister Heather planted 21 more flowers than Mia. How many flowers did they plant together?

91 flowers $35 + 21 = 56$ $35 + 56 = 91$

Larry has an 85 page reading assignment. He read 28 pages yesterday and 39 pages today. How many pages does Larry have left to read?

18 pages $28 + 39 = 67$ $85 - 67 = 18$

Claire found 55 seashells on the beach. Noah found 36 seashells. 28 of them were broken. How many unbroken seashells did they find together?

63 seashells $55 + 36 = 91$ $91 - 28 = 63$

The grocery store had 72 bags of potatoes. It sold 55 bags and brought in 36 more bags. How many bags of potatoes did the store have then?

53 bags $72 - 55 = 17$ $17 + 36 = 53$

In the library, 43 people are reading books. 26 people are using computers. 16 people are attending a book club meeting. How many people are in the library?

85 people $43 + 26 + 16 = 85$

Lesson 168

Tricky Word Problems

Solve each word problem. Use the space on the right for your work area.

The theater has 92 seats. 67 people came to see the play. 25 people bought their tickets on the spot. How many seats were empty?

25 seats $92 - 67 = 25$

Ron had 90 cents in his pocket. He bought a cookie for 12 cents and a candy bar for 25 cents. How much money did Ron spend in all?

37 cents $12 + 25 = 37$

Billy needs to solve 50 problems. His workbook has 75 pages. He has solved 27 problems so far. How many problems does Billy still need to solve?

23 problems $50 - 27 = 23$

Kyle caught 22 fireflies in the yard. Daniel caught 10 ladybugs. Then 6 fireflies flew away. How many fireflies did Kyle have then?

16 fireflies $22 - 6 = 16$

The pet store had 85 goldfish and 70 angelfish. It sold 57 goldfish and 36 angelfish. How many goldfish does the store have left now?

28 goldfish $85 - 57 = 28$

Jamie invited 15 friends to her birthday party. She took 46 pictures at the party. Her friend Ralph took 38 party pictures and sent them to her. How many pictures does Jamie have now?

84 pictures $46 + 38 = 84$

Lesson 169

Word Problems

Solve each word problem. Use the space on the right for your work area.

Larry read 125 pages of his reading assignment last week. He read 165 pages this week. How many pages did Larry read in all?

290 pages $125 + 165 = 290$

The pet store sold 257 goldfish this week. It has 184 goldfish left. How many goldfish did the store have at first?

441 goldfish $257 + 184 = 441$

Mr. Kim bought a television set and paid $398. He had $155 left. How much money did Mr. Kim have at first?

553 dollars $398 + 155 = 553$

The candy store sold 453 candies last week. It sold 328 candies this week. How many candies did the candy store sell altogether?

781 candies $453 + 328 = 781$

Ron collects stamps. He collected 323 flower stamps and 147 bird stamps. How many more flower stamps did Ron collect than bird stamps?

176 flower stamps $323 - 147 = 176$

The library had a book donation campaign. Two hundred sixty-nine books were donated last month. Fifty more books were donated this month than last month. How many books were donated in all?

588 books $269 + 50 = 319$ $269 + 319 = 588$

Lesson 170

Perimeter, Fractions & Symmetry

A. Calculate the perimeter of each rectangle.

50   **26**   **40**   **34**

B. Color in the shapes to find the missing numbers in the equivalent fractions.

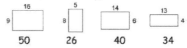
$\frac{1}{2} = \frac{4}{8}$ $\frac{4}{6} = \frac{2}{3}$

$\frac{6}{8} = \frac{3}{4}$ $\frac{3}{5} = \frac{6}{10}$

$\frac{1}{2} = \frac{2}{4}$ $\frac{2}{6} = \frac{4}{12}$

C. Draw the other half of each shape to make it symmetrical.

Lesson 171

Reading Bar Graphs

A. Use the bar graph below to answer the questions.

Books Read (bar graph — Number of Books vs Book Club Member: Max, Ron, Ava, Sam, Dan)

1. Who read the most books? **Ron**
2. Who read the fewest books? **Ava**
3. How many books did the book club read altogether? **30 books**
4. What is the title of this graph? **Books Read**

B. Use the bar graph below to answer the questions.

Tickets Sold (bar graph — Day of the Week vs Number of Tickets)

1. The most tickets were sold on **Wednesday**
2. The fewest tickets were sold on **Tuesday**
3. How many tickets were sold altogether? **190 tickets**
4. How many tickets were sold on Monday and Tuesday in all? **55**
5. How many more tickets were sold on Friday than Thursday? **5**
6. What is the name of the horizontal axis? **Number of Tickets**

Lesson 172

Bugs Bar Graph

The tally chart shows the number of bugs Stella and her friends found at the park. Make a bar graph to represent the data from the tally chart.

Butterfly	Beetle	Bee	Spider	Ladybug
卌 卌	卌 III	卌 卌 II	IIII	卌 卌 卌

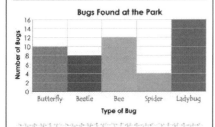

Bugs Found at the Park (bar graph — Number of Bugs vs Type of Bug)

1. How many bugs are there in all? **50**
2. How many bees and beetles are there in all? **20**
3. How many butterflies and spiders are there in all? **14**
4. How many fewer beetles are there than ladybugs? **8**
5. What is the name of the vertical axis? **Number of Bugs**

Lesson 173

Dessert Circle Graph

Adam asked his friends to vote for their favorite dessert. The tally chart shows their answers. Make a circle graph to represent the data from the tally chart.

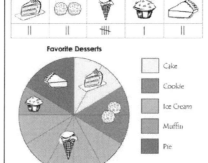

Favorite Desserts (circle graph)

Legend: Cake, Cookie, Ice Cream, Muffin, Pie

1. Which dessert received the most number of votes? **Ice Cream**
2. Which dessert received the least number of votes? **Muffin**
3. How many friends voted altogether? **12**

Lesson 175

Lemonade Line Graph

Ava has a lemonade stand. The line graph shows the number of lemonade cups sold each day. Use the graph to answer the questions.

Lemonade Sales (line graph — Number of Cups vs Day of the Week)

1. The least number of cups were sold on **Tuesday**
2. The most number of cups were sold on **Saturday**
3. How many cups were sold on Wednesday? **15**
4. How many more cups were sold on Saturday than Monday? **10**
5. How many fewer cups are sold on Tuesday than Thursday? **15**
6. How many cups were sold altogether? **145**
7. **Tuesday** and **Wednesday** sold less than 30 cups in all.

Lesson 176

Books Pictograph

The pictograph below shows the number of books Paul and his friends read during summer vacation. Use the graph to answer the questions.

Name	Number of Books
Paul	📖📖📖📖📖📖
Laura	📖📖
Stella	📖📖📖📖
George	📖📖📖📖📖

1. Who read the most number of books? **Paul**
2. Who read the least number of books? **Laura**
3. How many books did Laura and Stella read? **26**
4. How many more books did George read than Laura? **8**
5. How many fewer books did Laura read than Paul? **14**
6. Paul and George read **16** more books than Laura and Stella.
7. **Paul** and **Stella** read 40 books together.
8. How many books did they read altogether? **68**

Lesson 177

Apples Pictograph

The pictograph below shows the number of apples sold at the local grocery store over 4 months. Use the graph to answer the questions.

Month	Number of Apples Sold
August	🍎🍎🍎🍎🍎🍎🍎
September	🍎🍎🍎🍎🍎🍎🍎🍎
October	🍎🍎🍎🍎🍎🍎🍎🍎🍎🍎
November	🍎🍎🍎🍎

1. In which month were the most apples sold? **October**
2. In which month were the least apples sold? **November**
3. How many apples were sold in August? **35**
4. How many apples were sold in September? **40**
5. **15** more apples were sold in October than in August.
6. **15** fewer apples were sold in November than in September.
7. **25** more apples were sold in October than in November.
8. How many apples were sold altogether? **150**

Lesson 179

Division Squares

Each row and column is a division problem. Complete the squares.

18	3	6
2		2
9	3	3

32	4	8
8		4
4	2	2

24	4	6
6		3
4	2	2

48	8	6
6		3
8	4	2

20	2	10
5		5
4	2	2

36	4	9
6		3
6	2	3

16	2	8
4		4
4	2	2

27	3	9
9		3
3	1	3

30	2	15
5		5
6	2	3

We hope you had a great year with EP Math 3.

EP provides free, complete, high quality online homeschool curriculum for children around the world. Find more of our courses and resources on our site, allinonehomeschool.com.

If you prefer offline materials, consider Genesis Curriculum which takes a book of the Bible and turns it into daily lessons in science, social studies, and language arts for your children to learn all together. The curriculum also includes learning Biblical languages. Genesis Curriculum offers Rainbow Readers and a new math curriculum, A Mind for Math, which is also done all together and is based on each day's Bible reading. GC Steps is an offline preschool and kindergarten program. Learn more about our expanding curriculum on our site, genesiscurriculum.com.

Made in the USA
Middletown, DE
23 January 2021